POPULAR
GUITAR
MUSIC

POPULAR GUITAR MUSIC

Barry Pollack

PRENTICE HALL PRESS • NEW YORK

This book is available at a special discount when ordered in large
quantities. Contact Prentice Hall Press, Reference Group Special
Sales, 13th floor, 1 Gulf + Western, New York, NY 10023.

Published in 1987 by Prentice Hall Press
A Division of Simon & Schuster, Inc.
Gulf + Western Building
One Gulf + Western Plaza
New York, NY 10023

Originally published by Prentice-Hall, Inc.

PRENTICE HALL PRESS is a trademark of Simon & Schuster, Inc.

Library of Congress Cataloging-in-Publication Data

Pollack, Barry.
    Popular guitar music.

    Bibliography: p.
    Discography: p.
    1. Guitar—Instruction and study.   I. Title.
MT580.P747   1985   787.6'1'0712   85-6372
ISBN 0-13-685611-X

Manufactured in the United States of America

10   9   8   7   6   5   4   3   2

First Prentice Hall Press Edition

to My Family

ACKNOWLEDGMENTS

This book would not have been possible without the generous help of Peggy Pollack (patience and inspiration), Greg Carriere (transcriptions of guitar playing), Lisa Gordanier (music calligraphy), Lynette Miller (line drawings), Posey Gault and the Graphics Crew, A. Balcomb, Ronny Schiff, and the individuals and organizations at Cherry Lane, Columbia Pictures, Paul Simon Music, Web IV, Ice Nine, the Goodman Group, MPL, MCA, TRO, CTMP, Folklore Productions, Herzog and Strauss, Weiss Meibach & Bomser, Belwin/Mills, Almo/Irving, Gil, Bourne, and Warner Brothers, who have so kindly granted me permission to use the copyrighted song quotations included in this book.

With regard to the notation of string bends in Chapters 15 and 17, I use the same notation used by Michael Ihde, an instructor in the guitar department of Boston's Berklee College of Music. The system of notation used is drawn from *Country Guitar Styles* and *Rock Guitar Styles*, written by Michael Ihde and published by Berklee Press Publications.

Thanks also to E. T. G. of Freemont. And last, but certainly not least, I want to thank the authors of MicroPro's *WordStar*, Ashton-Tate's *dBASE II*, RoseSoft's *ProKey*, and Quarterdeck's *DESQ*, whose creativity has made my work so much easier and more enjoyable.

CONTENTS

PREFACE

Popular Guitar Music is a study of guitar playing as performed and recorded by Chuck Berry, Joan Baez, the Beatles, George Benson, the Clash, Leonard Cohen, Jim Croce, Steve Cropper, Fleetwood Mac, the Grateful Dead, Janis Joplin, Kansas, the Kinks, Lynyrd Skynyrd, Van Morrison, Joni Mitchell, the Rolling Stones, Paul Simon, The Who, Jerry Jeff Walker, Neil Young, and other guitarists of the past three decades.

Guitar playing skills are thoroughly explained, from the most basic chording and strumming techniques to advanced concepts of electric lead guitar and finger-style arrangements of melodies. Each technique is illustrated with transcriptions and references to available recorded guitar music.

Well-known recorded guitar parts are also used to illustrate *musical* ideas. Musical concepts are explained progressively from the fundamental (names of notes, reading simple rhythms, etc.) to the advanced (chord construction, complex rhythms, etc.). All musical concepts are presented with reference to, and in terms of *guitar* music.

Popular Guitar Music is a source book that can be referred to and enjoyed on many levels throughout a guitar player's musical development. The first three chapters are for readers who have never played before or who want to start fresh with the best possible techniques and attitudes. The mechanics and musical concepts of guitar playing are introduced and explained together.

Chapters 4 through 9 concentrate on finger picking and strumming accompaniment styles. The material in Chapters 10 through 13 helps to develop dexterity and strength in the hands and facility with musical ideas. Chapters 14 through 17 concentrate on single-note solo guitar, and they culminate in transcriptions of famous electric guitar solos as recorded by Chuck Berry, Buddy Holly, John Lennon, Keith Richards, and others. The next three chapters concentrate on systematically developing chord vocabulary and on applying guitar playing and musical skills to arranging *melodies* for solo performance.

Popular Guitar Music can be used by an individual player who wants to learn about music as well as about the guitar while also learning how to play the instrument accurately in the ways heard on recordings. The book is also useful for classroom teachers who want to give their students a legitimate music program while maintaining the students' interest by using guitar parts of famous recordings. Most chapters conclude with a set of exercises and projects.

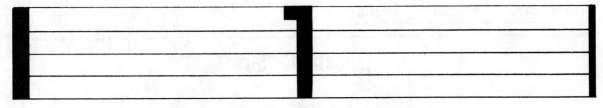

INTRODUCTION
TO THE GUITAR

The Parts of the Guitar

This section explains how the components of the guitar work together to produce musical sounds.

Tuning Gears

The tuning gears are attached to the *head,* which is at the end of the *neck.* The gears change the tension of the strings. Tightening a string raises its pitch; loosening a string lowers it. Locate the tuning gear attached to each string. Play any string and slowly turn the tuning gear attached to it, first one way, and then the other. Listen to the change in pitch as you turn the tuning gear.

Tuning the Guitar   Your ability to tune a guitar depends on the sensitivity of your ear and on the strength of your *tonal memory.* Anyone who enjoys music and who wants to play an instrument can learn how to tune the guitar accurately.

   If you have difficulty tuning your instrument, find someone who can teach ear training. Use an electronic tuner to tune your guitar. Electronic tuners analyze the note played by each string. A meter or set of lights indicates if the string is sharp, flat, or in tune. Playing on a well-tuned guitar trains the ear to recognize proper tuning. Electronic tuners make it possible for anyone to tune a guitar.

The Nut and Bridge

The strings are suspended between the *nut* and the *bridge.* The nut is located at the end of the neck near the head, and the bridge is found on the body of the guitar.

   Each string fits into different sized grooves in the nut. The thickest string lies in the widest slot. If the nut is too low or the slots too deep, the strings will buzz when played. If the nut is too high or the grooves too shallow, it will be difficult to press the strings against the frets.

   The bass end of the bridge is slightly higher than the treble end because the thicker strings need more room to vibrate without hitting the frets. The overall height of the bridge must be set correctly.

Nylon and Steel String Guitars

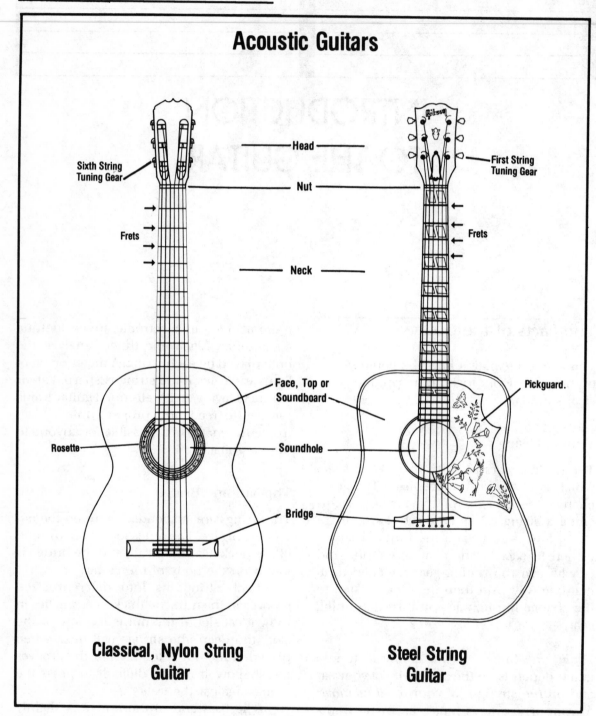

Acoustic Guitars

Head

Sixth String
Tuning Gear

First String
Tuning Gear

Nut

Frets

Frets

Neck

Face, Top or
Soundboard

Pickguard.

Rosette

Soundhole

Bridge

**Classical, Nylon String
Guitar**

**Steel String
Guitar**

Figure 1-1

Nylon and Steel Strings

Acoustic guitars are strung with either nylon or steel strings. A set of nylon strings consists of three treble strings—smooth nylon filaments—and three bass strings. The bass strings have nylon cores with soft metal wire wrappings. A set of steel strings usually contains two plain metal wire strings and four strings with wire wrappings around a metal core.

Nylon and steel string guitars are built of different materials to accommodate the different tensions and tonal qualities of nylon and steel strings. Nylon string guitars are made of thinner woods and more delicate hardware than steel string instruments. Do not put steel strings on a nylon string guitar because this will warp the neck, soundboard, or both and may literally pull the bridge off the face of the guitar. Nylon strings on a steel string guitar sound weak and toneless.

Decorations and Dots

The *rosette* surrounds the *soundhole* and is mostly decorative. *Position markers*, or *dots*, help locate frets in higher positions. Position markers identify odd-numbered frets—three, five, seven, and nine—and the twelfth fret. A special marker is placed at the twelfth fret. The twelfth fret is exactly halfway between the nut and the bridge. The note played at the twelfth fret sounds one octave above the open string.

Electric Guitars

In acoustic guitars, string vibration energy is transmitted through the bridge to the face of the guitar, which then vibrates the cavity of air formed by the face, back, and sides. In electric guitars, sound is produced by interaction between the vibrating strings and the pickups.

A cord connects the electric guitar to an amplifier. Wiring inside the pickups creates an electromagnetic field that surrounds the strings. An electric current passes from the pickups into the amplifier.

A vibrating string inside an electromagnetic field changes the *flux*, or intensity, of that field. The change in the electromagnetic field produced by the vibrating strings affects the flow of electric current in the pickups. The amplifier transforms the changes in current in the pickups into sound energy.

The toggle switch selects which pickups are on and off, and the volume and tone controls affect the sound as on a record or tape player.

Buying a Guitar

If you like the feel and sound of an instrument, you can learn to live with some of its faults or be willing to correct them. The neck of the guitar must not be excessively bent, bowed, or warped because this can make a guitar very hard to play and impossible to tune. Correcting a warped neck can cost more than the purchase price of a used guitar. Be sure also that the gears move smoothly without making abrupt changes in pitch. Look carefully at the frets on a used instrument. If the frets are so worn that you can't play clear notes, they will have to be replaced. Make sure that all the controls on an electric guitar work.

Holding the Guitar

Stylistic Considerations

Music is a performance art. Your posture while playing the guitar is a theatrical stance and a creative statement in itself. Each style of music has its own conventions of theatricality. Compare the visual appearances of Andres Segovia, Willie Nelson, Elvis Costello, and Eddie Van Halen as integral parts of their creative expression.

How you hold the guitar is based upon

A Solid Body Electric Guitar

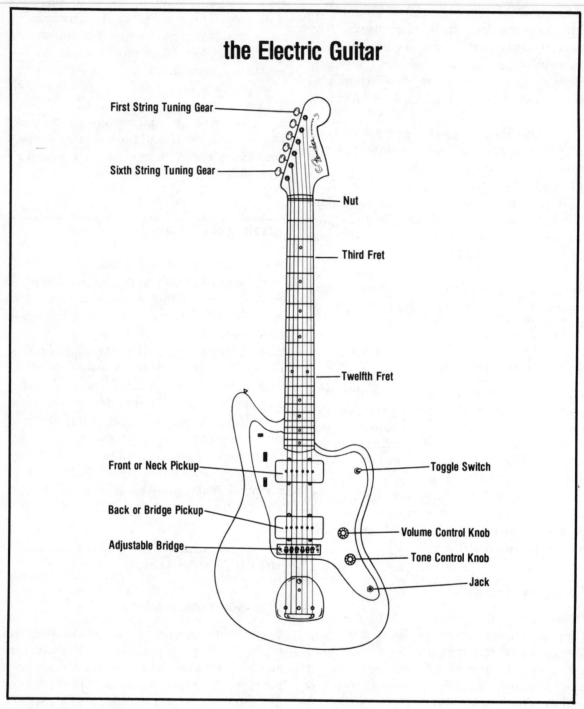

Figure 1-2

what is most comfortable and expressive. Watch other players, imitate them, and experiment on your own.

General Principles

Posture, breathing, relaxation, warmups, concentration, and setting and meeting goals are as important in playing the guitar as in any other physical activity. Whatever posture you assume, keep the following in mind:

1. Both hands should be free to move without the guitar slipping, dropping, or falling.
2. Keep the guitar upright, and avoid the temptation to look at the fretboard unless absolutely necessary.
3. If sitting, do not rest the left elbow on the left leg. This immobilizes the left hand and can cause serious backaches.

Fingers, Strings, and Frets

Hands and Fingers

The fingers of the left hand push the strings against the fretboard. The right hand strums or plucks strings, causing them to vibrate and produce sound. If you play the guitar left-handed, read "fretting hand" for "left hand" and "playing hand" for "right hand."

The fingers of the left hand are numbered one through four, and the fingers of the right hand are named *thumb* (t), *index* (i), *middle* (m), and *ring* (r). Numbered fingers form chord shapes on the fretboard; named fingers strum or pluck the strings to make them ring.

Strings

The first string is the thinnest and highest pitched string. The sixth string is the thickest and lowest pitched. This is the way strings are packaged and sold by all string manufacturers. The names of the strings from the low-sounding sixth to the high-pitched first are: *E—A—D—G—B—E.*

Grid Diagrams

Grid diagrams show the location of left hand fingers on strings and frets. Grid diagrams are found in Figure 1–3, in the chord charts of Figures 1–4 and 1–5, and throughout this book.

The six vertical lines of the grid stand for the six guitar strings. The line furthest right corresponds to the first or treble E string. The line furthest left corresponds to the low sixth string. The horizontal lines represent frets, and the top horizontal line represents the nut.

Numbers written on the vertical lines of the grid stand for left hand fingers. In Figure 1–3, the number 3 stands for the third finger as shown in the picture below the grid.

Higher and Lower

On the guitar, terms of comparison refer to changes in sound. Higher up the neck is movement toward the bridge and away from the nut, because notes sound higher in that direction. In Figure 1–3, the third finger is just below the third fret.

Chord Charts

These chords appear in every style of music. Do not press directly on top of the frets. A finger on top of the fret will muffle or mute the sound. Curve the fingers of the left hand at each knuckle. Point the fingers toward the fretboard, even when they are not pressing down a string.

All strings are part of a chord shape unless there is an x above the string in the chord diagram. For example, the low sixth string is not played in the D, D7, or D minor (Dm) chords. The top five strings are played in the D chords.

Guitar, Grid Diagram and Fretting Hand

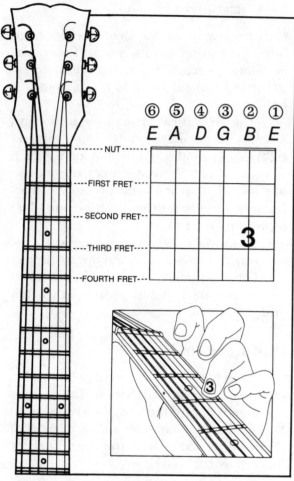

Figure 1-3

Numbers below the chord grids indicate alternative fingerings. For example, Chord Chart 1 shows two fingerings for the A major chord. The numbers on the grid show the A chord played with the first finger on both the third and second strings and the second finger on the second string. The alternate fingering shown below the grid uses the second, third, and fourth fingers. Figure 1–6 contains illustrations of the two ways to finger the A chord. There are more alternate shapes and fingerings in Figure 10–24.

In Chord Chart 2, F major and B minor (Bm) are shown with two chord shapes each. The *barre* (pronounced *bar*) chords are more challenging but more useful. A barre is formed by the first finger covering more than one string. A full barre is formed by placing the first finger across all six strings. A partial barre is formed by placing the first finger across two, three, four, or five strings. The barre chords in Chord Chart 2 are played with full barres.

Barre chords are movable. They can be played at any fret on the guitar neck. The system of naming barre chords played in

Chord Chart One

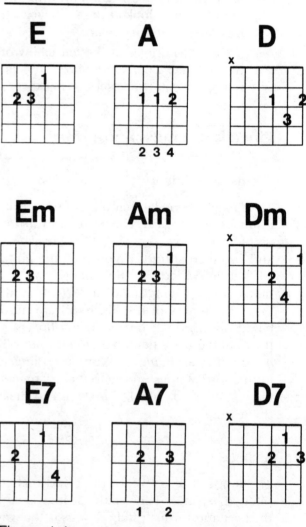

Figure 1-4

Chord Chart Two

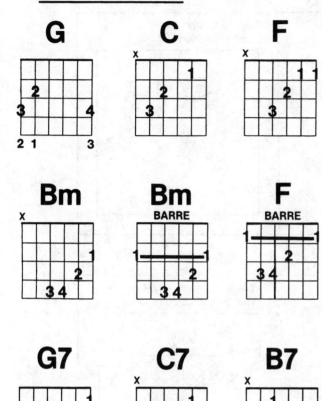

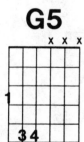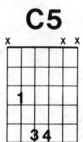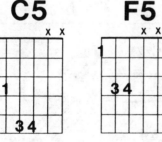

Figure 1-5

different positions is explained in Chapter 11.

The G5, C5, and F5 power chord shapes in the bottom row are also movable. The note under the first finger names the chords. These chord shapes are used in

heavy metal guitar playing. The first finger does not form a barre.

Chord Types

Every chord name contains a *root* and a *type*. The root of a chord is a note name; one of the first seven letters of the alphabet, sometimes modified by the symbols ♯ (sharp), or ♭ (flat). The chord type describes the sound or color of the chord. Type is indicated by letters or numbers following the root name of the chord.

The most common chord types are variations of one of three families of sounds: *major* (indicated by a root name only), *minor* (indicated by lower case m), or *seventh* (indicated by the number 7).

G major, G major chord, and G all mean the same chord. Em is an E minor chord. D7 is a D seventh.

The *fifth* chords in Figure 1–5 are neither major nor minor because they contain only roots and fifths (see Chapter 10 on chord construction).

Notation

Two systems of notation are used in this book: *tablature* and *staff*. Tablature notation, or *tab*, defines where notes are played on the neck of the guitar. In tab, numbers on lines represent frets on strings. In *staff* notation, symbols on lines and spaces indicate the actual pitch of each note.

Tablature and staff notation are read from left to right and notes are played in the order in which they are encountered. Notes written above each other are played at the same time.

Tab

The six horizontal lines in tablature represent the six strings of the guitar. The top line is the highest sounding first string. The lowest line is the lowest sounding sixth

Grid Diagrams and Pictures of the Left Hand Playing Chords

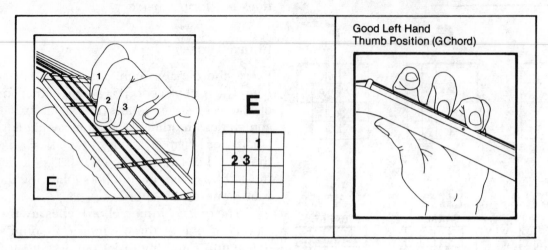

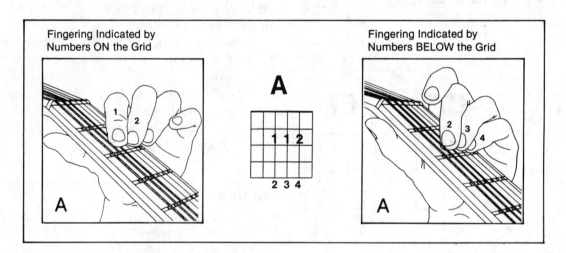

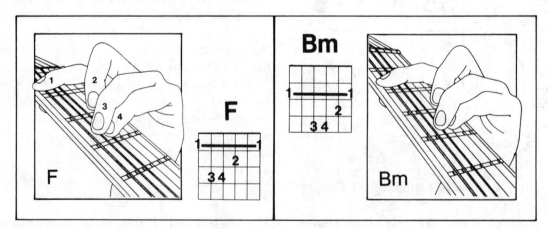

Figure 1-6

string. Numbers on the lines are frets. Zero (0) represents the open string. Play a string only if a number is on its line.

Figure 1–7 shows tab notation for the six open strings played one at a time, an E chord played one string at a time, and a strummed E chord.

Staff

The positions of the notes on the five-line staff show how the melody rises and falls. Notes placed low on the staff sound lower than notes written high on the staff. Figure 1–8 shows the notes of the six open strings in staff notation. Numbers in circles identify the strings. *Ledger lines* extend the range of the staff. The low sixth string is written using three ledger lines below the staff.

Bar lines divide the staff into measures. The number of beats in every measure of a song is usually the same. Each measure takes the same amount of time to play, re-gardless of the number of notes in the measures.

The shape of a note indicates how long it lasts. Simple note symbols last longer than complex note symbols. Duration symbols used in tab and staff are explained in Chapter 2.

Exercises and Projects

1. Play and name the strings in the following sequences:
   a. 6—5—4—3—2—1
   b. 1—2—3—4—5—6
   c. 4—5—3—4—2—3—6—1
2. Write the notes in Exercise 1 in staff and tab notation.
3. Play the E, A, and D major chords. What quality do all three chords have in common? Find a word that describes the common sound quality of the three

Tablature Notation

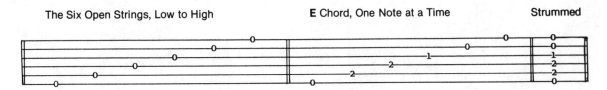

The Six Open Strings, Low to High   E Chord, One Note at a Time   Strummed

Figure 1-7

Staff Notation

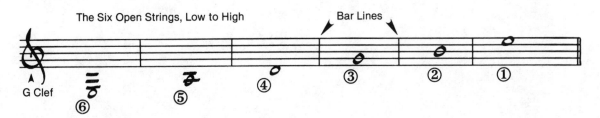

The Six Open Strings, Low to High   Bar Lines

G Clef   ⑥   ⑤   ④   ③   ②   ①

Figure 1-8

different major chords. Play Em, Am, and Dm. How would you describe the minor chord sound? The seventh chord sound? Learn to recognize the sound of major, minor, and seventh chords.

4. Each group of notes in Figure 1–9 is a chord shape. Name the chords.

Name These Chords

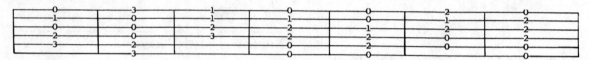

Figure 1-9

2

BASIC CONCEPTS OF MUSIC AND RHYTHM NOTATION

Melody, Harmony, and Rhythm

All music is made up of elements of melody, harmony, and rhythm. *Melody* is the rising and falling of single notes. *Harmony* is the vertical structure of two or more notes sounding at the same time. *Rhythm* is the sometimes even, sometimes jagged, heartbeat of musical sounds over time.

A goal of this book is to help guitarists identify the elements of melody, harmony, and rhythm in contemporary guitar music.

Units of Measurement

Intervals describe the difference in pitch between notes. Intervals are measured wth *half steps* and *whole steps*. A half step on the guitar is one fret. A whole step is two frets. Intervals are *melodic* or *harmonic*.

Combinations of long and short notes create rhythms. *Duration* describes how long a note or chord sounds. The *beat* is the unit of measurement of duration. Short notes last for fractions of a beat. Long notes last for several or many beats. *Tempo* is measured by the number of beats per minute.

The Musical Alphabet

Notes named by one of the first seven letters of the alphabet are called natural notes: A—B—C—D—E—F—G. Most adjacent natural notes are separated by a whole step. The exceptions are B and C, and E and F, which are separated by a half step. Learn the intervals between the natural notes. Fig-

Natural Note Intervals

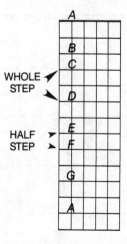

Figure 2-1

11

ure 2–1 shows the location of all the natural notes on the fifth string.

When two notes are a whole step apart, there is a note between them which is a half step above the lower note and also a half step below the higher note.

For example, A is the name of the unfretted fifth string. B, a whole step above A, is at the second fret of the fifth string. The note at the first fret of the fifth string is both a half step higher than A, called A sharp, or A♯, and also a half step lower than B, called B flat or B♭. Sharp means half step higher, and flat means half step lower.

A♯ and B♭ are two names for the same note. Similarly, the note on the fourth fret of the fifth string is called either C♯ or D♭. The symbols ♯ (sharp) and ♭ (flat) are called *accidentals*. Notes that are named with sharps and flats are called *chromatic notes*, or *chromatics*.

Rhythm Notation

Rhythm defines musical styles. A rhythm is composed of sounds of different durations.

A musical sound happens on the beat or at a specific place between beats. Rhythm notation is a system for writing down the beat locations of the sounds that constitute a rhythm.

The information in this section will help you to read rhythm notation so that you can understand and accurately perform the musical examples transcribed later in this book. Figure 2–2 shows some commonly used duration symbols. The tab symbols are indicated for a note played on the second fret of a string.

Counting and Playing Rhythms

These are the actions that must be coordinated in order to correctly count and play a given rhythm:

1. Tap a steady beat with your foot.
2. Count the beats one—two—three—four for each measure. (The examples in this chapter are illustrations of *common time*, or four beats per measure.)
3. Sound the rhythm by clapping or by

Simple Duration Symbols

SUMMARY OF RHYTHM NOTATION					
NAME	**STAFF**	**TAB**	**USED IN STAFF AND TAB**		**DURATION** (in beats)
			STRUM	**REST**	
WHOLE NOTE	o	②	◇	▬	4
HALF NOTE	♩	|②	♪	▬	2
QUARTER NOTE	♩	|2	↑	⌇	1
EIGHTH NOTE	♪	♪2	↯	7	1/2
SIXTEENTH	♬	♪2	↯	7	1/4

Figure 2-2

Simple Rhythms

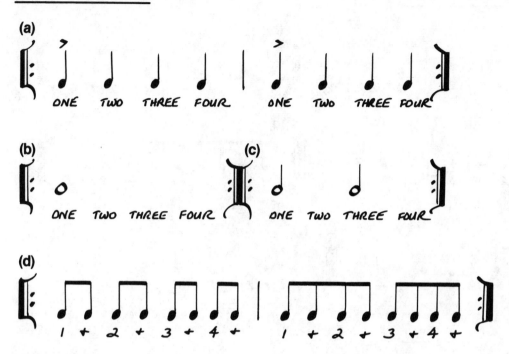

Figure 2-3

playing single notes or chords. The beat is unchanged by the sound of the rhythm.

Figure 2–3 contains simple rhythms that illustrate the fundamentals of reading, counting, and performing rhythms.

Quarter Notes Quarter notes get one beat each. Example *a* is two measures of quarter notes. The rhythm and beat are identical. Count each measure separately. Do not count "one—two—three—four—five—six—seven—eight."

Accents Notes placed under *accent signs* are played louder than the other notes in the rhythm. The first beat of each measure in Example *a* is accented. Accents create rhythmic shape and structure.

Long Notes The whole note in measure *b* lasts for four beats. The rhythm consists of one long sound. Count each beat. The half

notes in measure *c* get two beats each. The notes are played on beats one and three. Do not count the half notes "one—two—one—two."

Eighth Notes Written eighth notes are joined together by *beams* to make them easier to read. Keep in mind the following when counting eighth notes:

1. Tap slowly and pull the toe up with emphasis between each beat. The movement of the toe away from the floor (upbeat) is as important as the tap it makes when it lands on the floor.

2. Count one-and—two-and—three-and —four-and while tapping. Numbers are downbeats. The "ands" occur on the upbeat.

3. Emphasize the numbers (downbeats) or "ands" (upbeats) according to the accents in the rhythm.

4. The eighth note rhythm in Example *d* sounds twice as fast as the beat.

Rhythms with Ties

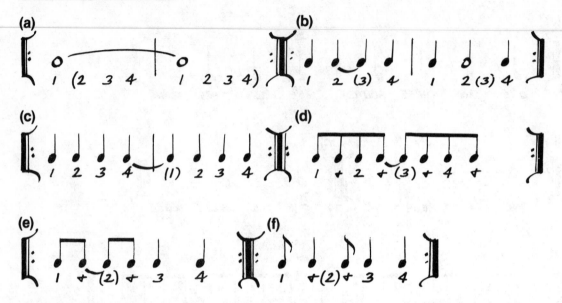

Figure 2-4

Ties and Dots Ties and dots are used to combine and extend the duration of notes. A tie is a curved line connecting two notes of the same pitch. The duration of the second note is added to the duration of the first. A dot after a note increases its time value by one half.

Figures 2–4 and 2–5 show examples of simple rhythms with ties and dots. Complex rhythms are built upon these kinds of simple patterns. The rhythms are sounded on the downbeats and upbeats not placed in parentheses. *Repeat signs* surround each example. Play each example twice without stopping.

The rhythm in Example *d* sounds twice as fast as the rhythm of Example *c*. Examples *e* and *f* are two ways of writing the same rhythm.

The dotted half note is equivalent to a half note tied to a quarter note. The dotted half note lasts for three beats. The two measures of Figure 2–5a sound the same.

The dotted quarter note is the equivalent of a quarter note tied to an eighth note. The dotted quarter note lasts for one and a half beats. The two measures of Figure 2–5b sound the same.

Rests and Strumming Symbols Silence plays an important part in music. Durations of silence are written with *rests*. Strumming symbols are used to show the duration of strummed chords in a rhythm pattern.

Rhythms with Dots

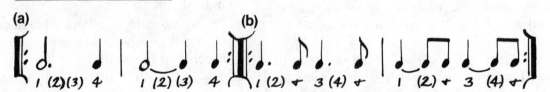

Figure 2-5

Strumming and rest symbols are the same in tab and staff.

Exercises and Projects

1. Intervals
   a. Name the notes a whole step above and below each of the following: C, E, G, B, F♯, A♭, B♭
   b. Name the intervals (whole or half steps) between these notes: C, D, E, F, G, A, B, C
   c. Determine how many half steps (frets) there are between the following pairs of notes: C and D; C and F; G and C; E♭ and A♭.

2. Notation
   a. Write out the scale in Exercise 1b in staff and tablature notation.
   b. The first fret is a half step above the open strings. Determine names of the notes at the first fret of all six strings.
   c. The third fret is a whole step above the first fret. Determine names of the notes at the third fret of all six strings.

3. Rhythms
   a. Clap or strum the rhythms in Figure 2–6.
   b. Write down rhythms heard on recordings of popular songs.

Rhythm Exercises

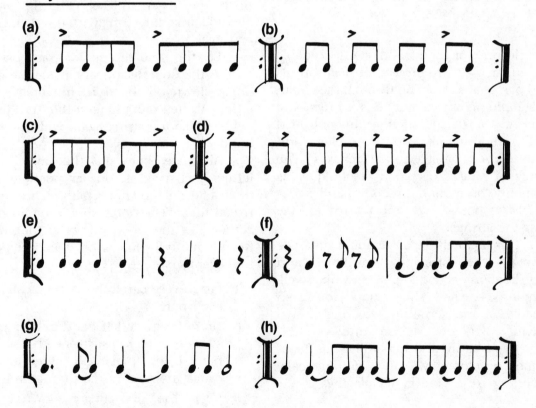

Figure 2-6

3

BASIC GUITAR
PLAYING SKILLS

Technique

The purpose of good technique is to enable the guitar player to project musical sounds and personal expression through the guitar. Developing good technique is a process of removing obstacles such as uncontrolled finger movements, slow muscles, and undeveloped or inaccurate reflexes. The principal idea of good technique is economy of motion in both hands: The fingers of both hands must learn to stay near the strings.

This chapter helps beginning guitarists develop the strength, flexibility, and coordination needed to play the guitar well. Simple exercises show how to listen creatively and critically to one's own playing. Work on exercises until you can play them easily and musically. The techniques developed will then automatically become part of your guitar playing.

Two Note Exercise

Fret the first string just below the first fret with the first finger of the left hand. Use the tip of the finger and keep the first finger curved. Strike the string with the right hand or a pick.

Let the note ring as long as possible. Just as the note disappears, place the third finger down on the third fret of the first string. At the exact moment the third finger lands, strike the string again with the right hand.

Alternate between the two notes, letting each ring as long as possible. Produce a flow of long notes with no breaks between them. The notes should be flush together, like the wood pieces of the guitar. Keep in mind the following when practicing this exercise:

1. Listen very carefully for the sustain of each note.

2. Do not remove left hand fretting pressure or touch the strings with the right hand before playing it, as either will cause the note to die prematurely.

3. Keep the first finger down while playing both notes. Reach all the way to the third fret with the third finger.

4. If the stretch between the first and third fingers is difficult or uncomforta-

ble, play the exercise in a higher position. The seventh and ninth frets, for example, are closer together than the frets near the nut. Move to lower positions as your fingers loosen and stretch.

5. Play on every string in every position.

Fingerpicking Tones

These exercises coordinate the right hand fingers and develop a variety of tone qualities for all fingerpicking styles. Right hand fingernails should be rounded and smooth.

Starting Position　Place the thumb, index, middle, and ring fingers on the sixth, third, second, and first strings, as in Figure 3–1a. Squeeze the strings: Push the thumb and fingers toward each other, as if making a gentle fist. Do not release the strings. Feel the resistance of each string under each finger.

Thumb Notes　The thumb points away from the hand and plays on its own section of the strings. This prevents the thumb and index fingers from getting in each other's way. Play the sixth string by pushing the thumb toward the other fingers. Control the motion of the hand so that only the thumb moves: The hand does not bounce and the index, middle, and ring fingers stay down on their strings, as in Figure 3–1b.

Play the sixth string again. Replace the thumb on the sixth string as quickly as possible so that the note is very short. The muscles which keep the fingers on or near the string must be developed along with the muscles which play the strings.

Index, Middle, and Ring Finger Notes　Place the right hand fingers in the starting position. Play the third string with the index finger. Let the third string note sustain while keeping the thumb, middle, and ring fingers planted firmly on their strings as in Figure 3–1c.

Play the second string with the middle finger. Keep the other fingers down on their strings. Play the first string with the ring finger: The unplayed fingers stay down. In this exercise, only one finger moves at a time. Unused fingers stay firmly on their strings.

Listen carefully to the *timbre*, or sound quality, of the notes. Change the angle formed by the fingers and the strings: Pull the fingers straight across the string or back toward the bridge. Use different parts of the fingertips; the nail only, combination of nail and flesh, or flesh only. Listen to the sound created by each change of angle and playing surface.

Finger Tone Exercise

(a) Starting Position

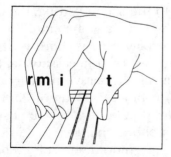

(b) Thumb Plays
the Sixth String

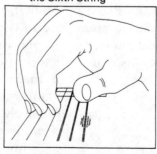

Index, Middle and Ring
Fingers Stay Down

(c) Index Finger Plays
the Third String

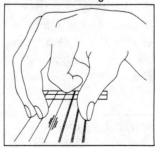

Thumb, Middle and Ring
Fingers Stay Down

Figure　3-1

Play near the bridge, over the soundhole, or near the bottom of the neck. Each spot on the string has its unique tone. Find a tone color you like and strive to make that sound consistently.

The Flatpick

Most electric guitarists, and many folk, bluegrass, and country and western acoustic guitarists, use a flatpick to strike the strings. A common and useful way to hold the pick is between the thumb and index finger, as in Figure 3–2.

Right Hand with Pick

Figure 3-2

The shape of the pick, its density, how it is held in the hand, and the angle and direction at which it strikes the strings all affect the sound of the picked string. Listen for the different tone each angle of attack produces. Experiment with different tones by playing near the bridge and over the soundhole.

A downstroke, indicated by ⌐ above a note or chord, is motion towards the floor. Upstrokes ∨ are made with motion away from the floor. Practicing up- and downstrokes on single strings improves all single note and rhythm guitar playing.

Playing Chords

This section focuses on three aspects of playing chords that all guitarists should strive to perfect.

1. *Clarity* Each chord is held so that every note is heard.
2. *Accuracy* Chord changes are swift and in time.
3. *Musicality* The right hand produces musical sounds.

Clarity

Sufficient pressure must be applied to the strings, the fingers must be as close as possible to the frets, and the finger that frets one string must not touch any other strings.

In order for a fretted note to ring clearly, the vibrating string must be held against a metal fret with enough force so that the string's motion of hundreds of oscillations per second is undisturbed. In time, calluses build up on the left-hand finger tips to protect them.

If the string buzzes while you are playing a fretted note, your finger may not be close enough to the fret. The further from a fret you place the finger, the harder you have to press to get a clean tone.

Accuracy

If it is not possible to place all the fingers of a chord down at the same time, put the fingers down according to the sequence in which the strings are played. In many styles, bass strings are struck before treble strings. When changing to a C chord put the third finger on the fifth string, add the second finger to the fourth string, and finally add the first finger to the second string, the order in which the strings will sound.

Be ready to play a new chord on the first beat of its measure. If necessary, let go of the previous chord early in order to change chords in time. In Figure 3–3, progressively shorter durations of rest are used to prepare for a chord change.

Simplify the movement of chord changes. Look for fingers which stay on the same note, or the same string, or which keep the same shape in the chord you are

Chord Changing Exercise with Rests

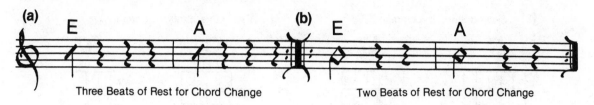

Three Beats of Rest for Chord Change   Two Beats of Rest for Chord Change

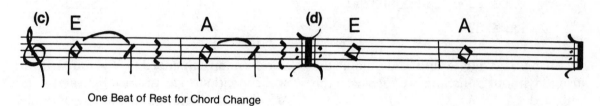

One Beat of Rest for Chord Change

Figure 3-3

playing and the chord to which you are changing.

Chord Changes with Notes in Common
Keep the finger firmly in place on the notes which are common to both chords. Lifting a finger off a note and then replacing it on the same note is wasted motion. Figure 3–4 shows several pairs of chords wth notes in common.

In *a*, the first finger stays on the second string first fret in Am and D7.

In *b*, the second finger stays on the fifth string second fret in E and B7.

In *c*, the first and second fingers can both stay down in Am and C.

Chord Changes with Strings in Common
Some chords share fingers which stay on the same string, but at different frets. Use

Chord Change Exercise: Common Notes and Fingers

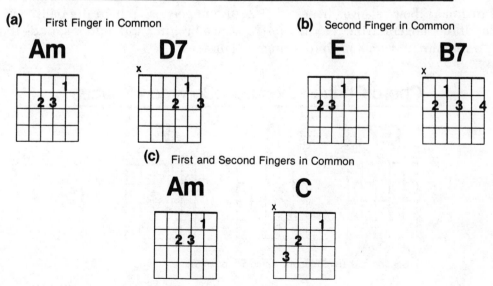

(a) First Finger in Common   **(b)** Second Finger in Common

Am   **D7**   **E**   **B7**

(c) First and Second Fingers in Common

Am   **C**

Figure 3-4

Chord Change Exercise: Common Strings

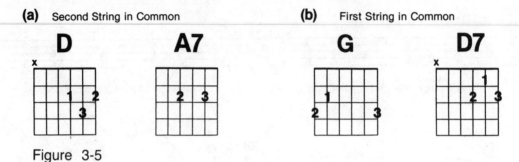

(a) Second String in Common   **(b)** First String in Common

Figure 3-5

the string as a guide and slide along the string without pushing it against the fretboard.

Chord Changes with Shapes in Common
Another way to improve chord changes is to look for fingers that keep a shape in both chords. Groups of fingers that have the same shape in two chords can and should move together as a unit when changing between the chords.

Figure 3–6 shows the C, G7, and the four string F chord. In all three chords the second and third fingers are one string and one fret apart. The second finger is one string higher and one fret lower than the third finger. When changing between C, F, and G7, make sure the second and third fingers maintain their relative shape.

The three fingers which form an E chord on the fifth, fourth, and third strings also form an Am chord on the fourth, third, and second strings. Change between E and Am without disturbing the shape of the left hand fingers.

Practice chord changes slowly in order to learn them correctly. When performing, maintain the beat and momentum of the music. The right hand leads and the left hand follows. The left hand must learn to keep up with the right.

Musicality

Vary the sound of a simple strum by using different strumming surfaces, strumming speeds, and strumming pressures. The palm side of the fingertips are flesh, and produce soft and mellow sounds when brushed across the strings. The backside of the fingertips contain the nails, which produce brighter and louder sounds than flesh surfaces.

Chord Change Exercise: Common Shapes

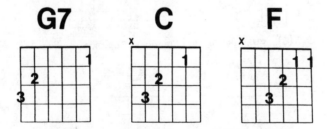

Second and Third Fingers: Same Shape in Three Chords

Figure 3-6

The flatpick produces bright strumming sounds. Variables which produce different flatpick sounds are the tension with which it is held in the fingers (loose or tight), and the angle at which the pick moves over the strings.

If the strings are strummed slowly, each string is heard individually before they all blend into one chord. Swift motion across the strings produces a single percussive chord.

The best strumming sound is produced by lightly brushing across the strings, as if brushing over a surface. Do not dig into the strings unless you want to bring out the sound of separate notes. Move the hand and arm gracefully in an arc over the strings. Aim for an even, well-balanced sound that contains both low and high strings.

Exercises and Projects

1. The two-note exercise at the beginning of this chapter called for a pair of long sustained notes with no gap between them. The two notes are played with the first and third fingers on the first string. In addition, use all combinations of left hand fingers: 1 and 2, 1 and 3, 1 and 4, 2 and 3, 2 and 4, 3 and 4.

2. Pick any chord you know reasonably well. Practice the change from that chord to every other chord shape you know. Some chord changes are easier than others. What makes a chord change easy or difficult, and how can you make a difficult chord change easier?

4

ACCOMPANIMENT STYLES
STRUMMING PATTERNS

The Accompaniment Style of Guitar Playing

This chapter begins a study of three types of accompaniments: strumming patterns, strumming patterns with bass notes, and fingerpicking patterns. In each, the left hand plays chords while the right hand maintains a steady rhythm. The study of accompaniment guitar styles develops playing skills and helps to discover and understand the elements of music—melody, harmony, and rhythm—in different styles of guitar playing. Transcriptions of recorded guitar playing illustrate the techniques and concepts.

Strumming Patterns

Quarter Note Strums

A quarter note strum is one strum on every beat. A strum on each beat provides strong momentum. The exact number of strings hit depends upon how much sound you want. The more strings you strike, the fuller and louder the sound of the accompaniment.

Strums on every beat can be heard clearly in "Get Back" by the Beatles, "My Generation" by the Who, and "Roxanne" by the Police. In these examples, each beat is accented equally.

A simple variation is produced by accenting the second and fourth beat. Listen to "Midnight Hour" by Wilson Pickett, "Get Off My Cloud" by the Rolling Stones, and "Taxman" and "Sergeant Pepper's Lonely Hearts Club Band" by the Beatles for examples of strong accents on the second and fourth beats.

Eighth Note Strums

Eighth note strumming patterns are heard in many styles of music. Eighth note patterns are played with either alternating down and up strokes or with all downstrokes. Two downstrokes per beat requires twice as much arm movement as alternate down- and upstrokes.

An eighth note strumming pattern is made more interesting by striking the bass strings on the first and third beats and the treble strings on the second and fourth

Eighth Note Strumming Patterns with Accents and Rests

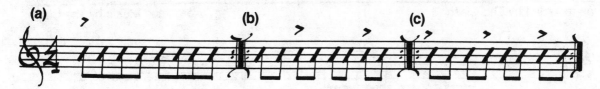

Figure 4-1

beats. Listen to the Eagles' "Peaceful Easy Feeling" and the Beatles' "I Will" for examples of this effect.

Patterns with Accents and Rests

Figure 4–1 shows eighth note strumming patterns with accents and rests. The accents in Example 4–1a fall on the naturally strong beats. In Example *b*, the accents are on the second and fourth beats. In Example *c*, the accents are unevenly spaced.

Figure 4–1b is heard in John Lennon's "Ballad of John and Yoko." In this song, the guitarist strikes only the treble strings on the accented beats. In "Watching the Detectives," Elvis Costello muffles the bass strings on the first and third beats of a similar rhythm, a typical reggae pattern.

Variations in eighth note strumming pattern are created by omitting some of the strums, as in Examples 4–1d and 4–1e. The following transcriptions are recorded examples of eighth note strumming patterns with rests.

The rhythm in the Kinks' "You Really Got Me" is played with all downstrokes. Use barre G and F chords. The rhythm is repeated in higher positions.

The Clash's "Should I Stay or Should I Go?" is played with all downstrokes and open position chords.

The guitar parts in Figure 4–4 demonstrate more complex use of eighth note strums and rests. The Paul Simon introduction begins with the eighth note rhythm of Guitar 1. Use the four string chords shown in the grid diagrams. Except for the first A,

You Really Got Me (Eighth Note Rhythm with Rests)

as recorded by The Kinks   Words and Music by Ray Davies

Use All Down Strokes

Figure 4-2
Used by permission of Jay Boy Music Co.

Should I Stay or Should I Go? (Eighth Note Rhythm with Rests)

as recorded by The Clash

Words and Music by The Clash

Use All Down Strokes

Figure 4-3

Me and Julio Down by the School Yard (Rhythm with rests)

as recorded by Paul Simon

Words and Music by Paul Simon

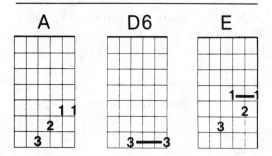

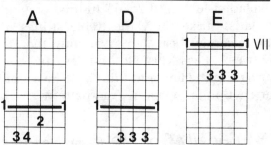

Figure 4-4

Copyright ©1971, Paul Simon.

chords change on upbeats in this pattern. The A and E are played with first finger partial barres and the D6 chord is played with the third finger across the top four strings at the seventh fret.

Guitar 2 plays full barre chords. The D and E barre chords are played with the same shape. D is at the fifth fret and E is at the seventh fret, indicated by the Roman numeral VII next to the E chord grid. The eighth note x's in Guitar 2 indicate muffled strums. Finger the chord shape with the left hand and release the pressure so that no notes ring clearly. Squeeze the chord with the left hand to produce the accented eighth note strums on the second and fourth beats.

The introductions to Elvis Costello's "Less Than Zero," AC/DC's "Highway to Hell," Michael Jackson's "Billy Jean," the Scorpians' "Hurricane," and "Owner of a Lonely Heart" by Yes are more examples of eighth note patterns with rests.

Quarter and Eighth Note Strums Combined

The strumming patterns in Figure 4–5 are played with a constant up and down strumming motion; downstrokes on the downbeats and upstrokes on the upbeats. The right arm moves down and up and hits the strings as indicated by the rhythm notation.

The arm moves downward past the strings without sounding them on the third beat in measures c and d. This motion prepares the arm for the next upbeat, which is

played with an upstroke. To practice the patterns, stay on any chord and repeat each rhythm until it becoms automatic. Then choose any two chords and play one measure of each while maintaining a single pattern.

Figure 4–6 is the introduction to The Eagles' "Take It Easy." The unevenly accented strumming pattern is contrasted with sustained chords. The long chords are rapidly arpeggiated, indicated by a wavy line in the lower staff.

When the first beat of a chord change is tied to a previous beat, change to the new chord on the strum to which the chord change is tied. In Figure 4–7a, the fourth upbeat of the first measure is an A chord, even though the A chord symbol appears at the beginning of the second measure.

In Figure 4–7b the changes to F and G are played on upbeats. Compare this rhythm to the sound produced by changing to F and G on downbeats.

Songs with clearly recorded quarter and eighth note strumming patterns in-

Strumming Patterns with Combined Durations and Ties

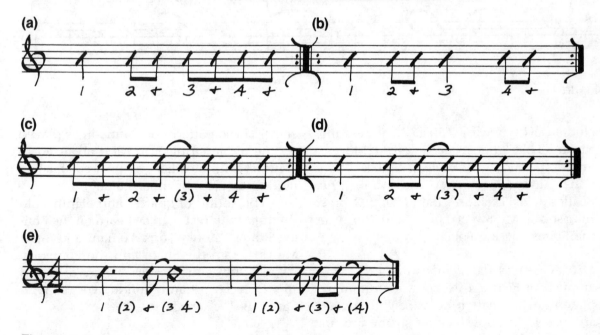

Figure 4-5

Take It Easy (Strumming Patterns, Introduction, Two Guitars)

as recorded by The Eagles   by Jackson Browne & Glenn Frey

Figure 4-6

Two Measure Rhythms with Early Chord Changes

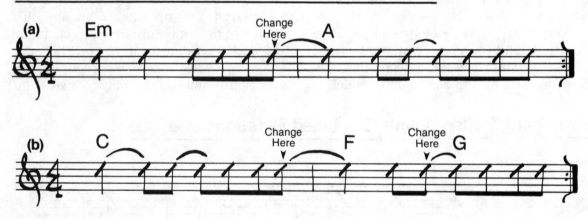

Figure 4-7

clude David Bowie's "Space Oddity," the Kinks' "Lola," Bob Seger's "Night Moves" (middle section), the Rolling Stones' "You Can't Always Get What You Want," the Beatles' "A Day in the Life," George Harrison's "My Sweet Lord," and "Born in the Fifties" by the Police.

Mixed Quarters and Eighths with Rests Example *a* of Figure 4–8 shows a strumming pattern with quarter notes, eighth notes, and ties. In Example *b* chord strums are cut

short. These patterns are sometimes played on the treble strings only and are used to contrast with steadier rhythms established by drums, bass, or other guitars.

The sound of quarter and eighth note rhythms with rests can be heard on the Rolling Stones' "Honky Tonk Woman" and "Start Me Up," Sam the Sham and the Pharaohs' "Wooly Bully," the Beatles' "The Word" and "It's Only Love," and Men at Work's "Who Can It Be?"

Strumming Patterns with Combined Durations and Rests

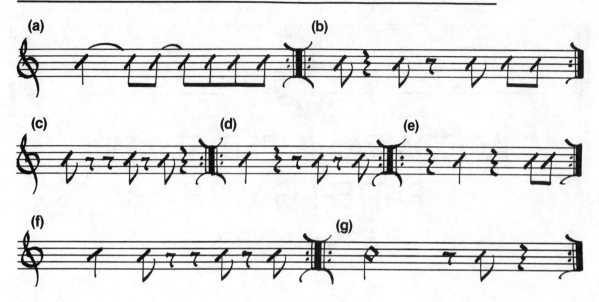

Figure 4-8

5

ACCOMPANIMENT STYLES: PATTERNS WITH BASS NOTES

Bass and Chord Accompaniment Patterns

Guitar accompaniments become more interesting when bass notes are added to strumming patterns. By adding bass notes, the guitarist can play a bass part as well as carry the rhythm and chord changes of an accompaniment. Accompaniment patterns which use individual bass notes in addition to chord strums are called *bass and chord* or *bass/strum* patterns.

John Lennon, Bob Dylan, Joan Baez, and other guitarists of the 1960s who popularized the bass and chord style were continuing a tradition of guitar accompaniment that was first popularized on a national scale by Riley Pucket and Mabelle Carter in the 1920s and 1930s.

Bass Notes

The Root Note

Each note in a chord contributes to its sound. There is a note in every chord which,

by itself, sounds most like the entire chord. That strongest note is the root of the chord, the note which also names the chord.

Primary and Secondary

Bass notes are usually played on the first and third beats of a measure. The first bass note to sound is called the primary bass note. The primary bass note is determined by the name of the chord, the root of the chord played on one of the bass strings.

Other bass notes are called secondary bass notes. The secondary bass note is another root, or a third or fifth of the chord (see Chapter 10: Major Scale Intervals and Chord Construction). In Figure 5–1, the primary and secondary bass notes are identified by the strings on which they fall in each chord shape.

In most bass and chord patterns, the guitarist alternates between the primary and secondary bass notes on the first and third beats and strums the treble strings on the second and fourth beats.

There is one primary bass note with two or more secondary bass notes in every

Primary and Secondary Bass Notes

CHORD	BASS STRINGS		
	PRIMARY	SECONDARY	ALTERNATE SECONDARY
E, E7, Em	⑥	④	⑤
A, A7, Am	⑤	④	③, ⑥
D, D7, Dm	④	⑤	③
G, G7	⑥	④	⑤
C, C7	⑤	④	③, ⑥
F (4 string)	④	③	⑤
F (6 string)	⑥	④	⑤

Figure 5-1

chord. For example, the most commonly used secondary bass note of the E chord is found on the fourth string. The note on the fifth string of the E chord is an alternate secondary bass note. Use your ear to find the secondary bass notes which sounds best in a given accompaniment.

The primary and secondary bass notes of a chord are determined by the name of the chord, regardless of the chord type. Sixth string E is the primary bass root note for the E, Em, and E7 chords. Memorize the primary and secondary bass notes for all the chords you use. Learn the locations of primary and secondary bass notes of all new chords. The primary and secondary bass notes are also used in fingerpicking patterns.

Recorded Examples

The Beatles often used bass and chord styles in their acoustic guitar playing. "Rocky Raccoon" is an example of bass notes added to simple quarter note strum. The beginning of "Yesterday" is also a root bass note and an eighth note strumming pattern, as transcribed in Figure 9–9.

Janis Joplin used the primary bass note of the G chord and combinations of quarter and eighth notes strumming patterns in her introduction to "Me and Bobby McGee," as shown in Figure 5–2.

A slash in a chord name indicates a chord with a specific bass note. C/G is called C slash G, C with G in the bass, or C over G.

To change smoothly between the chords, keep the third and fourth fingers on the sixth and first strings; move only the second and first fingers. The open fifth string should not sound in the C/G chord. To mute the fifth string, let the third finger of the left hand lean over and dampen the fifth string.

Alternation between G and C/G is also heard in Bob Dylan's "Takes a Lot to Laugh, a Train to Cry," recorded on the *Concert for*

Me and Bobby McGee (Bass/Chord Pattern, Introduction)

as recorded by Janis Joplin

by Kris Kristofferson & Fred Foster

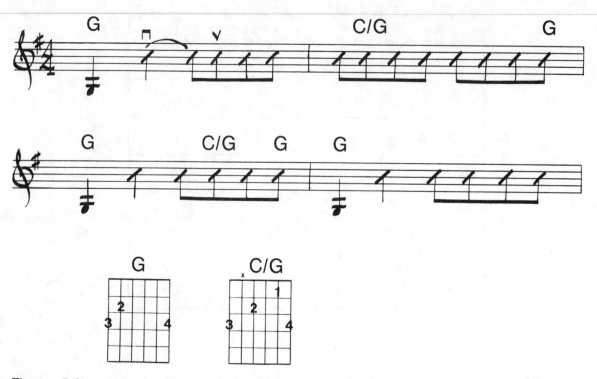

Figure 5-2

Bangladesh album and in the guitar accompaniment of Dan Fogelberg's "Leader of the Band" and in Paul Simon's "Kathy's Song."

Alternating Bass Patterns

The bass notes in Figure 5–3 are found on the strings indicated by numbers in circles in the staff notation. For example, measures *a* through *d* are played under a G chord. In each measure the primary bass note is on the sixth string and the secondary bass note is on the fourth string.

Measure *e* is an alternating bass pattern in Am with the fourth string as secondary bass note. In measure *f* the sixth string is used as the secondary bass. The measures at *g* show alternating bass notes applied to a common progression.

Right Hand Technique

Play bass and chord patterns with the right hand fingers or with a flatpick. If you use the fingers, play bass notes with the thumb and strum treble strings with the index or middle fingers. You can use the thumb to play the bass notes and also to strum chords although it is harder to coordinate the rhythm pattern at faster tempos with only the thumb.

If you play with a pick, tighten the pick in the fingers when you strike the bass strings, and let the pick give sightly when strumming the chords. Holding the pick too tightly when strumming the chords produces a harsh and unpleasant sound. Relax the wrist when brushing across the strings. All downbeats are played with downstrokes and all upbeats are played with upstrokes.

Alternating Bass Patterns

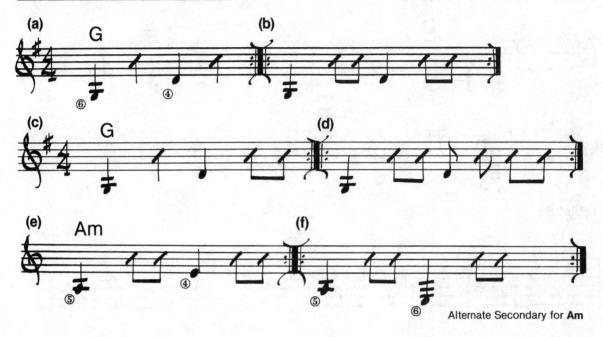

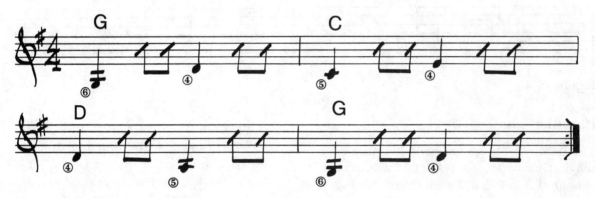

Figure 5-3

Aim to strike the three treble strings on the strumming portion of bass and chord patterns. The fewer strings you hit, the softer the sound; the more strings you hit, the louder the sound. Strike more or fewer strings according to the sound you wish to project.

Bass Runs

Bass runs connect chord changes. Any song accompaniment that uses alternating bass notes is enhanced by using bass runs. A bass run is a series of bass notes that ends with a change to a new chord. Figure 5–4 shows bass runs from D to G.

Any notes can be used for a bass run, provided they lead musically to the root of the next chord. Figure 5–5 shows a bass run that ends on a G chord but that starts from four different chords.

The introduction to Johnny Cash's "I Walk the Line" consists entirely of alternating bass notes and bass runs.

Bass Runs from **D** to **G**

Tablature

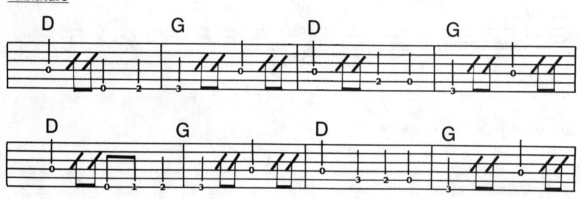

Figure 5-4

Hammer-Ons

The hammer-on is a left hand technique for playing individual notes. The hammer-on, executed by a left hand finger hitting a string onto the fretboard, connects two ascending notes. The hammer-on is commonly used to add notes to bass and chord guitar styles.

Hammer-on Notation and Technique The hammer-on is indicated by a curved line, or arc, connecting an ascending pair of notes. Figure 5–6 shows a hammer-on added to a C chord in a bass and chord strumming pattern.

The notes in parentheses at the beginning of the first measure are held down throughout the exercise. Play the first measure as follows:

1. Finger the C major chord and lift the second finger off the fourth string.

2. Strike the open fourth string and let it ring for a full beat. It may take some extra attention to clear the open fourth string while holding down the rest of the C chord.

3. Hammer to the second fret with the left hand second finger. Slam the tip of the finger against the fourth string at the second fret. Do not let the knuckles of the left hand collapse. The fourth string E note will sound by the action of the left hand alone.

4. Follow the timing of the music.

The second and third measures of Figure 5–6 show how to add the hammer-on to an alternating bass and chord pattern. The

Bass Runs to G from Different Chords

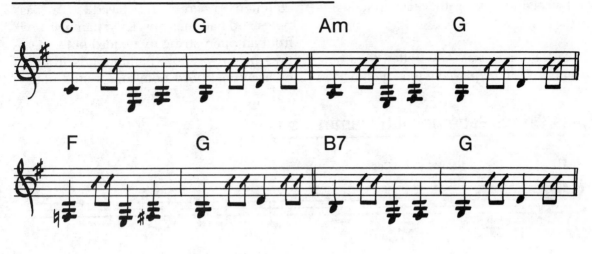

Tablature

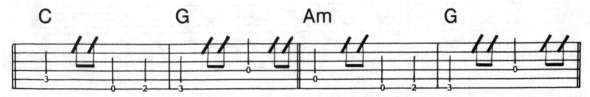

Figure 5-5

Hammer-on Exercise, with Chord Shape

C Chord notes:
Hold down throughout

Figure 5-6

open fourth string note and the hammer-on to the second fret together take exactly one beat.

Using Hammer-Ons   Any fretted bass note of a chord can be played with a hammer-on from its open string. Figure 5–7a shows a common progression played with bass notes and hammer-ons. Each hammer-on is from an open string to a chord note. Measures *b* and *c* show hammer-ons from an open string chord note to a fretted note.

Bass/Chord Patterns with Hammer-ons

Figure 5-7

"Ripple"

The acoustic guitar introduction in the Grateful Dead's "Ripple" uses bass runs and hammer-ons to outline the melody of the song. Notes written in parentheses in Figure 5–8 are played very softly, as in the recording. Most of the individual notes fall on chord shapes. Play notes and chords on downbeats with downstrokes and notes and chords on upbeats with upstrokes.

Ripple (Bass/Chord Patterns With Hammer-ons and Bass Runs)

as recorded by The Grateful Dead   Words and Music by Robert Hunter and Jerry Garcia

Notes in Parentheses ( ) are played very softly.

Figure 5-8
©1971 by Ice Nine Publishing Co., Inc. Used by permission.

Ripple (Tab)

Figure 5-9

Exercises and Projects

1. Figure 5–10a shows a hammer-on exercise using the first and third fingers on the first and third frets of all six strings. Figure *b* shows hammer-ons on the first string with all combinations of left hand fingers in first position. Apply each left hand combination in *b* to the six-string exercise in *a*.

2. Analyze the Grateful Dead introduction. Identify root bass notes, alternating bass notes, bass runs, and hammer-ons in each measure.

Hammer-On/Combinations Exercise

Figure 5-10

6

ACCOMPANIMENT STYLES: FINGERPICKING PATTERNS

Fingerpicking patterns are used extensively in acoustic guitar styles. Paul Simon, John Denver, John Fahey, Bert Jansch, Ralph McTell, Gordon Lightfoot, James Taylor, Dan Fogelberg, Doc Watson, John Lennon, Paul McCartney, Stevie Nicks, Steve Howe, Ry Cooder, Keith Richards, Jimmy Page, and Eddie Van Halen have recorded songs using fingerpicking patterns.

In fingerpicking styles, strings are plucked individually by right hand fingers. The right hand thumb traditionally plays on the bass strings. The thumb plucks the strings downward. The index, middle, and ring fingers pluck upwards on the treble strings. Most fingerpicking patterns fall into two styles: *arpeggios* and *three-finger picking*.

Arpeggios

An arpeggio consists of the notes of a chord played in sequence. In the simplest arpeggio, the notes of a chord are played one at a time from the lowest to highest. On the guitar, the thumb plays a bass string and the index finger plays the third string, the middle finger plays the second string, and the ring finger plays the first string. The thumb most often plays root notes, as in the Rolling Stones' "Play with Fire" in Figure 6–1. The notes of an arpeggio can be played with a flatpick.

The Kinks' "Tired of Waiting for You" uses a contrast between strummed power chords, G5 and F5, and individually picked arpeggio patterns on the top three strings. The arpeggios are played on extensions of the rhythm chords, G6 and Fadd9 (see Chapter 18: Chord Vocabulary).

Figure 6–3 shows the syncopated arpeggio pattern Joan Baez used in "Diamonds and Rust." The thumb plays bass notes on the first downbeat, the second upbeat, and on the fourth downbeat of each measure.

A syncopated arpeggio pattern is heard in the repeated *coda* (ending) of The Eagles' "Hotel California." Two guitars play high position treble string chord arpeggios in harmony. A transcription is published in the May 1984 edition of *Guitar for the Practicing Musician*. Other guitar arpeggios are heard throughout the Police's "Every Breath You Take."

38

Play with Fire (Simple Arpeggio Pattern)

as recorded by The Rolling Stones

Words and Music by Nanker Phelge

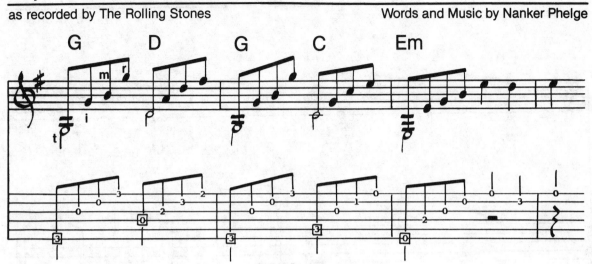

Figure 6-1

Tired of Waiting For You (Arpeggio Pattern, Two Guitars)

as recorded by The Kinks

Words and Music by Ray Davies

Figure 6-2

Diamonds and Rust (Syncopated Arpeggio Pattern)

as recorded by Joan Baez   by Joan Baez

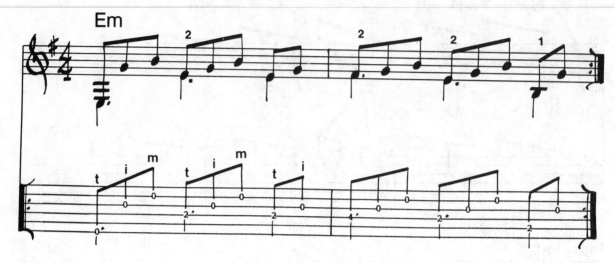

Figure 6-3
©1975 by Chandos Music ASCAP.

Three-finger Picking

Three-finger picking developed in the 1920s and 1930s when guitarists attempted to imitate the sound of blues, ragtime, and stride piano. Since then, three-finger picking has become the most popular and widespread fingerpicking guitar style.

In three-finger picking, the thumb plays alternating bass notes while the index and middle fingers play treble notes. The steady rhythm of the thumb on the bass strings dominates the three-finger picking patterns. The index and middle fingers can play on any treble strings, and are not assigned to specific strings as in the arpeggio patterns.

Pinch and Roll

Treble notes are played at the same time as bass notes or between bass notes. A pinch is a treble string note played on the beat with a bass note. A roll is a treble note played off the beat, between bass notes. All three-finger picking patterns are combinations of pinches and rolls. Playing the measures of Figures 6–4 (staff) and 6–5 (tab) develops the coordination necessary to play three-finger picking pinch and roll patterns. Practice each measure until it can be played easily.

In the pinch and roll exercise, the index and middle fingers play on the second and first strings. The thumb alternates between the fourth and fifth strings of a C chord. Repeat each measure accurately at several tempos.

Measure *a* is a pinch on the first beat only. The middle finger plays the first string at the same time the thumb plays the primary bass string on the first beat. Let the first string sustain for four beats.

Measure *b* shows a first string pinch on the first and third beats. Measure *c* shows a pinch on all four beats: The middle finger plays the first string every time the thumb plays a bass note. Measures *d,* e, and *f* show a pinch on various beats played by the index finger. The index finger plays on the second string.

Measure *g* is a roll on the first beat only. The middle finger plays the first string on

Three-Finger Picking: Pinch and Roll Exercise: C Chord

Thumb Plays all Notes with Stems Pointing Down

Figure 6-4

Three-Finger Picking: Pinch and Roll Exercise (Tab)

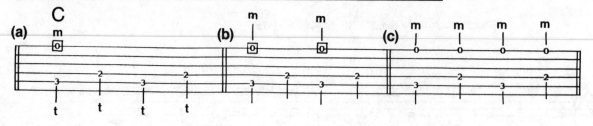

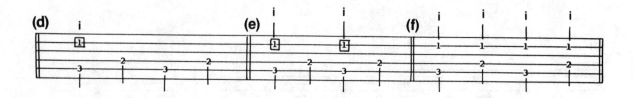

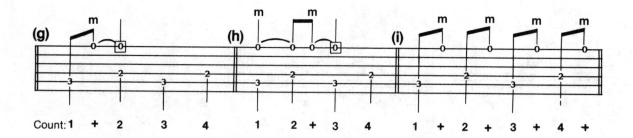

Figure 6-5

the first upbeat. The thumb plays evenly on every downbeat. The treble note falls between the first two bass notes.

Measure *h* is a combination of a pinch on the first beat and a roll on the second beat. Measures *i, j,* and *k* show a roll on every beat. Measure *k* is a pattern called the *three-finger roll.* The index and middle fingers alternate rolls on the second and first strings. The fingers play in this sequence: thumb—index—thumb—middle.

Play the three-finger pattern with any chord progression. Adjust the thumb so that

it plays primary and secondary bass notes. Practice at different tempos. At a moderate to fast tempo, the three-finger roll produces a pleasant "bubbling brook" accompaniment.

"Landslide"

Fleetwood Mac recorded "Landslide" with the pattern shown in Figure 6–6. This is a variation of the three-finger roll in which a treble note is not played on the first upbeat. To play with the record, put a capo on the fourth fret.

Keep in mind the following when practicing "Landslide:"

1. The time between the first two bass notes is a full beat. Do not rush the second bass notes. The time between the first two notes is twice the time between any other notes in the pattern.

2. The thumb always plays the fifth and fourth strings.

3. The index finger plays on the third string and the middle finger plays on the second string.

Listen to John Denver's recording of "Leaving on a Jet Plane" for another example of this pattern. Similar patterns can be heard on the Beatles' recordings of "Julia" and "Mother Nature's Son."

"Dust in the Wind" by Kansas is an ex-

Figure 6-6

Landslide (Picking Pattern: Three Finger Roll Variation)

as recorded by Fleetwood Mac

Words and Music by Stevie Nicks

Capo Fourth Fret to Play with Record

ample of a three-finger roll with a pinch added to the first beat. A transcription can be found in the July 1984 issue of *Guitar for the Practicing Musician*. See the bibliography for other sources of transcriptions.

Patterns with Three Bass Notes

The pattern in Figure 6–7 can be heard on Paul Simon's recording of "The Boxer" and on John Denver's recording of "Take Me Home, Country Roads."

Patterns with Hammer-Ons

Hammer-ons can add interest to picking patterns. Keep in mind the following when practicing the E pattern in Figure 6–8a.

1. The left hand alone plays second string C♯.
2. The fourth finger hammers onto the second string at the same time the thumb play the fourth string.

3. Anticipate the second string hammer-on by resting the thumb on the fourth string immediately after playing the sixth. This way, the thumb is ready to release the fourth string when the left hand plays the hammer-on.
4. To hear the correct rhythm, play the pattern striking every note with the right hand.

Listen to Keith Richards' acoustic guitar playing in "Prodigal Son" on the *Beggar's Banquet* album and to Bob Dylan's playing "Buckets of Rain" on the *Blood on the Tracks* album for examples of similar hammer-ons added to fingerpicking patterns. Listen to the Rolling Stones' "Factory Girl" for a pattern similar to Figure 6–8b.

This chapter only introduces the basic concepts and techniques of fingerpicking the guitar. See the bibliography for references to other sources which explore fingerpicking patterns.

Picking Patterns with Three Bass Notes

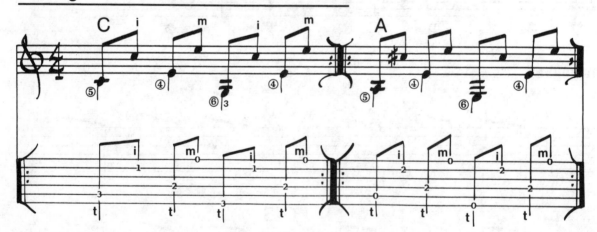

Figure 6-7

Picking Patterns with Hammer-ons

Figure 6-8

7

MAJOR SCALES, TIME SIGNATURES, AND SIXTEENTH NOTES

The Major Scales

Scales describe the notes found in melodies, licks, and chords. The major scales are the yardsticks with which other scales, all chords, and all progressions are measured and built. For example, every type of A chord (A major, A minor, A7, and so on) can be defined in terms of the notes of the A major scale.

Scale Degrees

The notes of a scale are identified by their position in the scale. The position of a note is called its scale degree. The first note of every scale is called the root. The root is also the first degree of the scale. The second note of the scale is the second degree. The row of note-names in Figure 7–1 is the C major scale. The root, or first degree, of the C scale is C. The second degree of the C scale is D.

Patterns of Intervals

The sound of a scale—major, minor, chromatic, and so on—is created by the pattern of intervals between its notes. All major scales have the same pattern of intervals. In Figure 7–1, the row of numbers called scale degrees shows the intervals (whole step or half step) between the notes of the major scales.

The interval between all adjacent scale degrees is a whole step, except between the 3rd and 4th degrees and the 7th and 8th degrees. The 3rd and 4th degrees and the 7th and 8th degrees are a half step apart.

The Notes of the Major Scales

To find the notes of any major scale, preserve the major scale pattern of intervals. For example, the notes of the C major scale are derived as follows:

1. The interval from the root to the 2nd degree of all major scales is a whole step. The note a whole step above C is D. D is the 2nd degree of the C scale.
2. The interval from the 2nd to the 3rd degree is a whole step. A whole step above D is E. E is the 3rd degree of the C scale.

46

Major Scales

	SCALE DEGREES							
1 Whole	**2** Whole	**3** Half	**4** Whole	**5** Whole	**6** Whole	**7** Half	**8**	
C	D	E	F	G	A	B	C	
G								
D								
A								
E								
B								
F#								
Gb								
Db								
Ab								
Eb								
Bb								
F								

Figure 7-1

3. The interval from the 3rd to the 4th degrees is a half step. The note a half step above E is F. F is the 4th degree.

4. The 5th degree of the scale is G, a whole step above F.

5. The 6th degree is A, a whole step above G.

6. The 7th degree is B, a whole step above A.

7. The 8th degree, or octave C, is a half step above B.

These are the rules for finding notes of the major scales:

1. Each degree is named with the next letter of the alphabet above the previous degree.

2. Do not leave out letter names. For example, the 6th degree of the G scale is E. The 7th degree is F♯, not G♭, which leaves out the letter name F from the scale.

3. Do not duplicate letter names in a scale. The 3rd degree of F major is A. The 4th is B♭, not A♯, which duplicates A.

4. Major scales may contain either sharps or flats, not both.

5. The octave is always the same letter as the root.

6. The fifth degree of each scale is the root of the next lower scale in Figure 7–1. The scales are in order by the *cycle of fifths*.

Time Signatures

The time signature is a pair of numbers written at the beginning of a piece of music. The upper number of a time signature indicates the number of beats in each measure and the lower number tells what kind of note gets one beat.

Common Time, 4/4

Many commonly used rhythms have four beats in each measure. Four beats of quarter notes per measure is called common time. The letter C is sometimes used to indicate common time, as in Figure 7–2.

Cut Time, 2/2

In cut time, there are two beats per measure and each half note gets one beat. Whole notes get two beats and quarter notes each get half a beat. The published music of many songs is written in cut time.

Common Time and Cut Time

4/4 or Common Time

Counting in Cut Time, or 2/2

Figure 7-2

Counting in 3/4 and 6/8

Three Beats Per Measure
Quarter Note Gets One Beat

Six Beats Per Measure
Eighth Note Gets One Beat

Figure 7-3

3/4 and 6/8 Time

In 3/4 time, each measure lasts three beats and quarter notes get one beat. Songs in 3/4 include: "Goodnight Irene," "Amazing Grace," "Morning Has Broken" (Cat Stevens), "Manic Depression" (Jimi Hendrix), "The Times They Are A-Changin'" (Bob Dylan), "New Amsterdam" (Elvis Costello), and "Lucy in the Sky with Diamonds" (the Beatles).

In 6/8 time there are six beats in each measure and each eighth note gets one beat. Since quarter notes always last twice as long as eighth notes, quarter notes get two beats, and dotted quarter notes get three beats. Examples of songs in 6/8 include: "House of the Rising Sun," the Beatles' "You've Got to Hide Your Love Away," and Iron Maiden's "Phantom of the Opera."

In 3/4 time, a measure of eighth notes is counted as three groups of two. In 6/8 time, a measure of eighth notes is counted as two groups of three.

Sixteenth Notes

A sixteenth note has half the duration of an eighth note. In 4/4, sixteenth notes get a quarter of a beat. Four beats divided into sixteenth notes are counted one-e-and-a; two-e-and-a; three-e-and-a; four-e-and-a. The foot taps the beat on the numbers only, as in Figure 7–4. Example *c* shows several ways of writing a syncopated rhythm in which the first part of each beat lasts three times longer than the second part.

To count a difficult sixteenth note pattern, rewrite it with the duration of each note doubled. The resulting pattern will be easier to read. A rhythm can also be simplified by counting eighths: Eighth notes get a full beat, sixteenth notes get half a beat, and there are eight beats in the measure.

Counting Sixteenth Note Rhythms

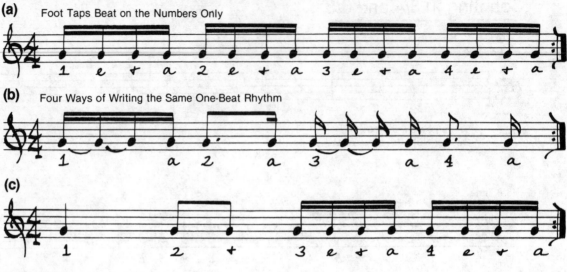

Figure 7-4

Exercises and Projects

1. Memorize the major scale pattern of intervals.
2. Finish filling in the major scale chart in Figure 7–1. Compare your work to the correctly filled in chart in Figure 7–6 at the end of this chapter.
3. Write out the major scales in staff notation.

4. Play one octave of each major scale in first position and write it out in tablature.
5. Memorize the notes of all twelve major scales.
6. Play the rhythms in Figure 7–5. If necessary, rewrite them with the time values of each note doubled, or count in eight.

Exercise: Counting Rhythms (Sixteenth Notes)

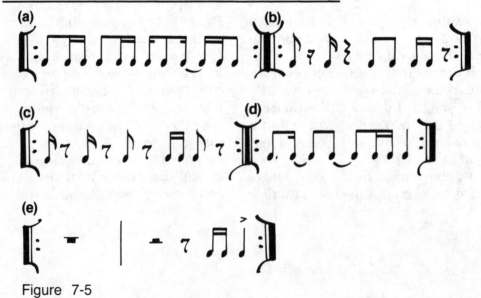

Figure 7-5

SCALE DEGREES							
1	2	3	4	5	6	7	8
C	D	E	F	G	A	B	C
G	A	B	C	D	E	F#	G
D	E	F#	G	A	B	C#	D
A	B	C#	D	E	F#	G#	A
E	F#	G#	A	B	C#	D#	E
B	C#	D#	E	F#	G#	A#	B
F#	G#	A#	B	C#	D#	E#	F#
Gb	Ab	Bb	Cb	Db	Eb	F	Gb
Db	Eb	F	Gb	Ab	Bb	C	Db
Ab	Bb	C	Db	Eb	F	G	Ab
Eb	F	G	Ab	Bb	C	D	Eb
Bb	C	D	Eb	F	G	A	Bb
F	G	A	Bb	C	D	E	F

Figure 7-6

8

NOTES ON THE FRETBOARD: CHANGING CHORDS

Know the names of the notes in order to communicate intelligently with other musicians and also to create bass runs, bass lines, riffs, and solos. Knowing the location and names of all the notes on the guitar enables a guitarist to construct chords and to find fingering patterns for scales.

Begin the task of learning all the notes of the fretboard with natural notes in first position. Natural notes are named without sharps or flats. First position includes the open strings and the first four frets.

Natural Notes in First Position

The location of the notes is indicated by numbers in the staff notation of Figure 8–1. The numbers in circles stand for strings. Numbers next to the notes represent left hand fingers. In first position, the first finger plays first fret notes, second finger plays second fret notes, and third finger plays third fret notes. For example, on the sixth string, E is the open string, F is played with the first finger on the first fret and G is played with the third finger on the third fret.

The grid diagram on the bottom of Figure 8–1 also shows the location of natural notes in first position. These are the important guidelines for playing the scale:

1. As with all scales, sustain each note until the next one sounds.
2. Keep fingers down. Leave the first finger on first fret F when adding the third finger to third fret G.
3. Each finger stays as close as possible to its fret and points toward the strings in preparation for playing its note.
4. When descending, lifting fingers off the strings too early causes ghost notes. Lift fingers to play the next lower note just as the right hand is about to strike the string.
5. Practice the scale slowly enough so that every note is played evenly, both ascending and descending. There should be no break in tempo when changing strings.
6. Name the notes as you play them.

Use any of the following right hand patterns:

Natural Notes in First Position

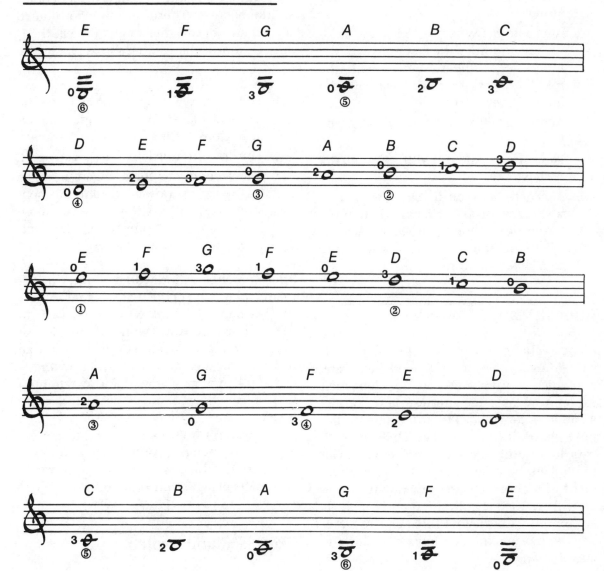

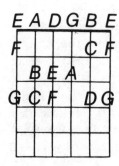

Numbers in Circles Indicate Strings; ⑥ is Low E String.
Small Numbers Next to Notes are Left Hand Fingers and Frets.

Figure 8-1

1. Play every note with the thumb, including the notes on the treble strings.
2. Alternate between the index and middle fingers. Strike the first note with the index finger, the next note with the middle finger, the third note with the index finger, and so on.
3. Alternate between the middle and ring fingers.
4. Play every note with a flatpick downstroke.
5. Alternate between flatpick down- and upstrokes. Keep a strict alternation between down- and upstrokes regardless of whether the next note is on the same or a different string.

Chord Change Exercises

A chord change is a coordinated set of individual finger movements. Smooth, accurate, and quick chord changes are possible when each finger takes the shortest path from its location on one chord to its location on the next chord. These exercises show how to coordinate and quicken the movement of all the fingers by practicing each finger movement of a chord change separately.

In Figure 8–2 both the D and G chords are played with the first three fingers. Practice the movement of each finger within the chord change:

1. The first finger makes a short straight motion across the strings.
2. The second finger makes a large motion from one edge of the neck to the other.
3. The third finger moves between adjacent strings at the same fret. Make no unnecessary motion. The finger should not pass the target note and have to come back to it.

Two fingers should leave their notes at the same time, and land on the next set of notes simultaneously. These are the coordinated movements of two fingers at a time in the D and G chord change, as shown in Figure 8–2:

1. The first two fingers move from the treble strings, two strings apart, to adjacent bass strings.
2. The first and third fingers spread apart.
3. The second and third fingers move as far apart as possible from adjacent strings. The third finger moves more slowly so that both fingers land on their notes at the same exact time.

After practicing individual finger movements, play the D chord and visualize how the left hand will look when it changes to the G chord. Look at the hand, but do not move any fingers. When you have an image of what the fingers will look like in the G chord, change very slowly and carefully to G. Control the motion of each and every finger.

These routines can be used to perfect any chord change. Work slowly and accurately so that the correct movement is made automatically through repetition.

Exercises and Projects

1. Memorize the location and names of natural notes in first position.
2. Figure 8–3 shows the names of the notes on all the strings of the E, A, D, and G chords. The note on the third string of the E chord is called G♯ and not A♭ because the notes of the E major scale are named with sharps (see Chapter 10 on chord construction). Name the notes on all the strings of all chords you play.

Chord Change Exercise: Finger Combinations

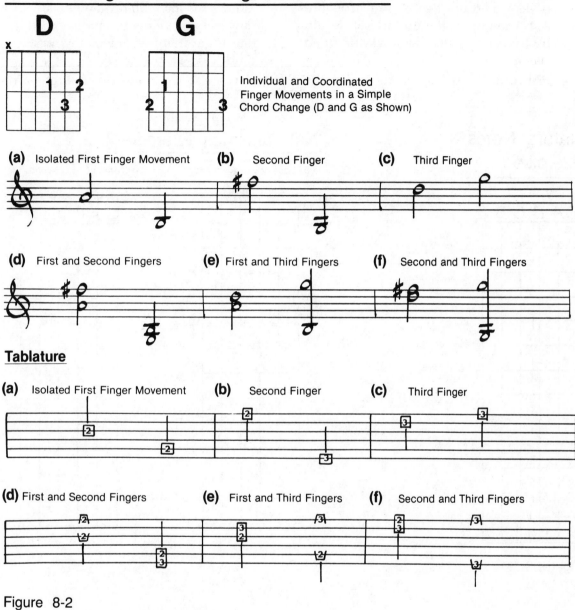

Individual and Coordinated
Finger Movements in a Simple
Chord Change (D and G as Shown)

Figure 8-2

Notes in Chords: E A D G

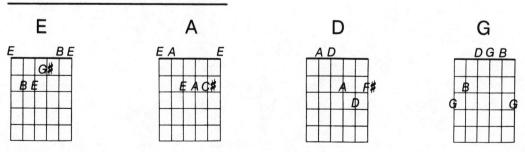

Figure 8-3

3. Fill in the location of all the natural notes up to the twelfth fret in Figure 8–4. The note at the twelfth fret should be the same letter name as the open string.

4. Figure 8–5b shows the names of the notes at the seventh fret. Figure 8–5a shows the location of all A notes. Select any fret and name the notes on all the strings at that fret. Select any note and find it on all the strings.

5. Memorize the notes on the fretboard.

Natural Notes Exercise 1

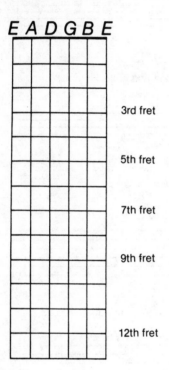

E A D G B E

3rd fret

5th fret

7th fret

9th fret

12th fret

Figure 8-4

Natural Notes Exercise 2

(a) Location of All A Notes

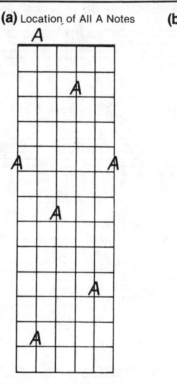

A

(b) Notes at the Seventh Fret

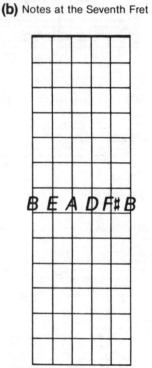

B E A D F♯ B

Figure 8-5

9

MORE ACCOMPANIMENT PATTERNS AND MELODIC BASS LINES

Accompaniments in 3/4 and 6/8

Strumming Patterns

The simple 3/4 strumming patterns in Figure 9–1 can be clearly heard in Cat Stevens' "Morning Has Broken."

In 6/8 time, eighth notes get one beat and sixteenth notes get half a beat. You can hear clear 6/8 strumming patterns in John Lennon's guitar playing on "You've Got to Hide Your Love Away." Unusual chord types are created by adding the first string G note to D, F, and C major, as in Figure 9–2.

Arpeggio Patterns in 6/8

Figures 9–3 and 9–4 show an arpeggio pattern in 6/8 in the chord progression to the "House of the Rising Sun." Accents are created by the thumb and ring fingers playing on low and high notes.

Starting in measure 9, the last note of each measure is played by the thumb. This bass note substitutes in the pattern for a

Strumming Patterns in 3/4

Figure 9-1

You've Got to Hide Your Love Away (Excerpts, Strumming Patterns in 6/8)

as recorded by The Beatles   Words and Music by John Lennon & Paul McCartney

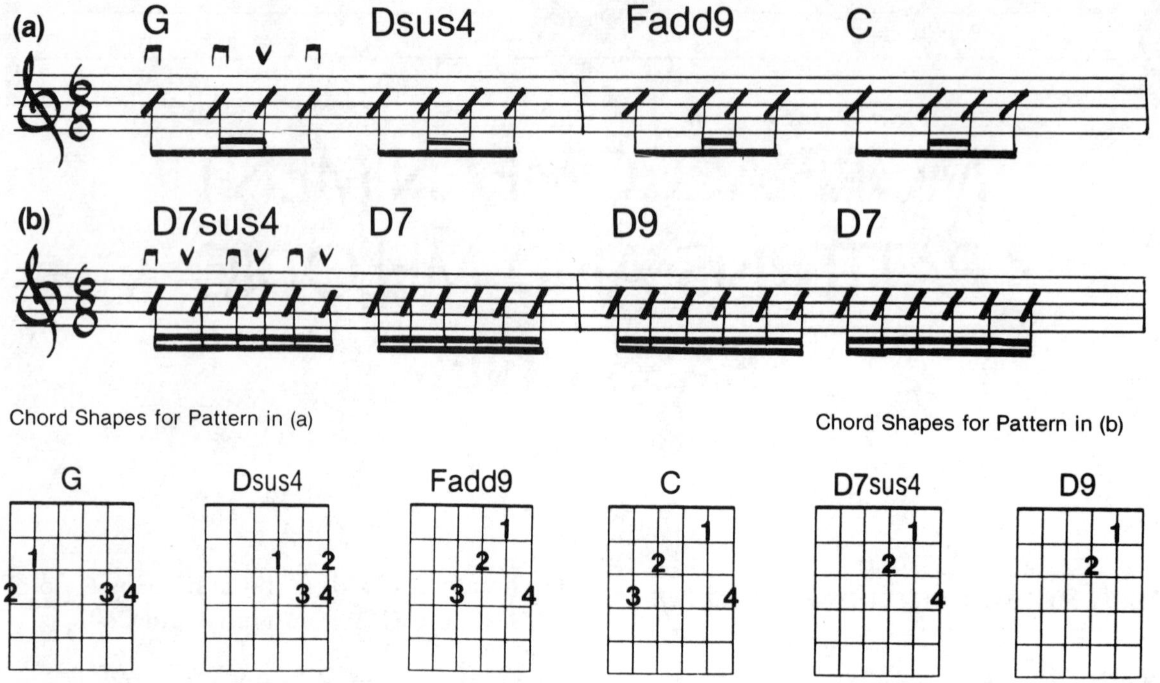

Figure 9-2

note played by the index finger on the third string. The added bass notes create bass runs between the chords.

Melodic Bass Lines

A bass line is created by the bass notes in bass/chord chord or fingerpicking patterns. Melodic bass lines are created by using nonchord tones in addition to the primary and secondary bass notes.

Bass runs and bass lines differ: Bass runs are usually played within half a measure, while bass lines can span several measures. The effect of a bass run is to connect a

pair of chords. The effect of a bass line is to unify several chords in a progression. The bass notes in the first four measures of Figure 9–3 form an ascending bass line.

"Mr. Bojangles"

Bass notes on the first beat of the first five measures of Figure 9–5 form a descending bass line. The bass line follows the notes of the C major scale. Bass lines that fall on a major scale are called *diatonic bass lines*.

Many of the chords have several names. C/B (C major with a B note in the bass) is sometimes called CMaj7. C/A in the third measure is sometimes identified as a

House of the Rising Sun (Arpeggio Pattern in 6/8)

Figure 9-3

House of the Rising Sun (Tab)

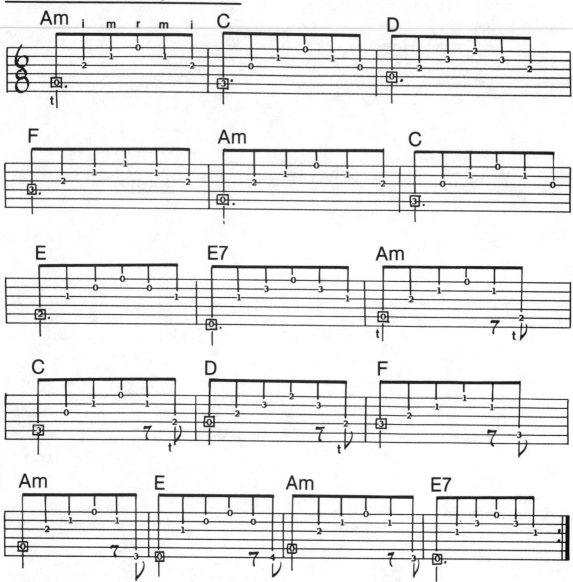

Figure 9-4

Mr. Bojangles (Strumming Pattern with Bass Line)

as recorded by Jerry Jeff Walker

by Jerry Jeff Walker

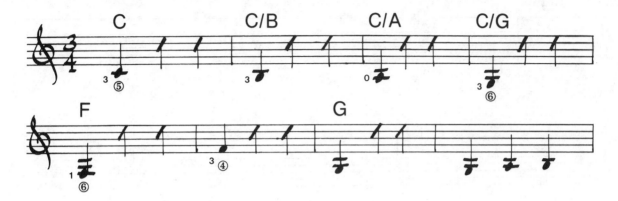

True Pitch: Key of D, Capo II

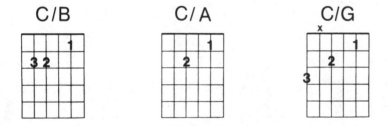

Figure 9-5

C6 or Am7 chord. C/G in the fourth measure is also called Am/G, Am7, or Am7/G. F is a six string barre chord. The sixth string F is part of the bass line. The chord names in Figure 9–5 include the notes of the bass line.

The ascending bass run in the eighth measure contains the same notes as the descending bass line in measures 2, 3, and 4. Paul Simon uses a similar descending diatonic bass line in 3/4 time in his song "America." Listen to "For No One" by the Beatles for another example of a diatonically descending bass run.

Bass Lines and Bass Runs with Picking Patterns

Figure 9–6 shows a picking pattern with a bass line in the first measure and a bass run

in the second. G/F♯ is a G chord with sixth string, second fret F♯ in the bass.

"Needle and the Damage Done"

Figure 9–7 is a transcription of Neil Young's guitar playing from "Needle and the Damage Done." The guitar work contains some unusual chord changes and subtle strumming techniques. A bass line connects the chords in the first four measures. Measures 2, 3, and 4 contain a chromatically descending bass line.

Keep in mind the following when playing this guitar part:

1. Accent the first beat bass note in the first four measures.

2. Through the fourth measure, single

Picking Pattern with Bass Line and Bass Run

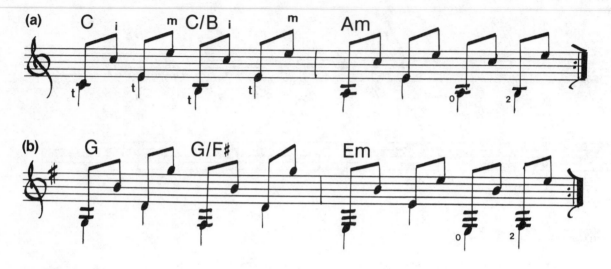

Tablature

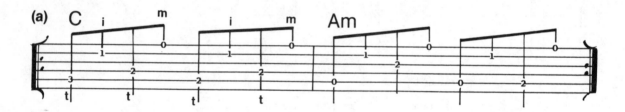

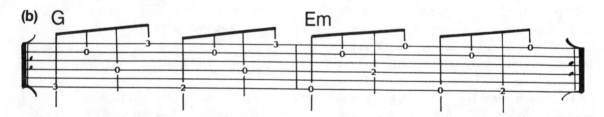

Figure 9-6

Needle and the Damage Done (Strumming Patterns with Bass Lines)

as recorded by Neil Young

by Neil Young

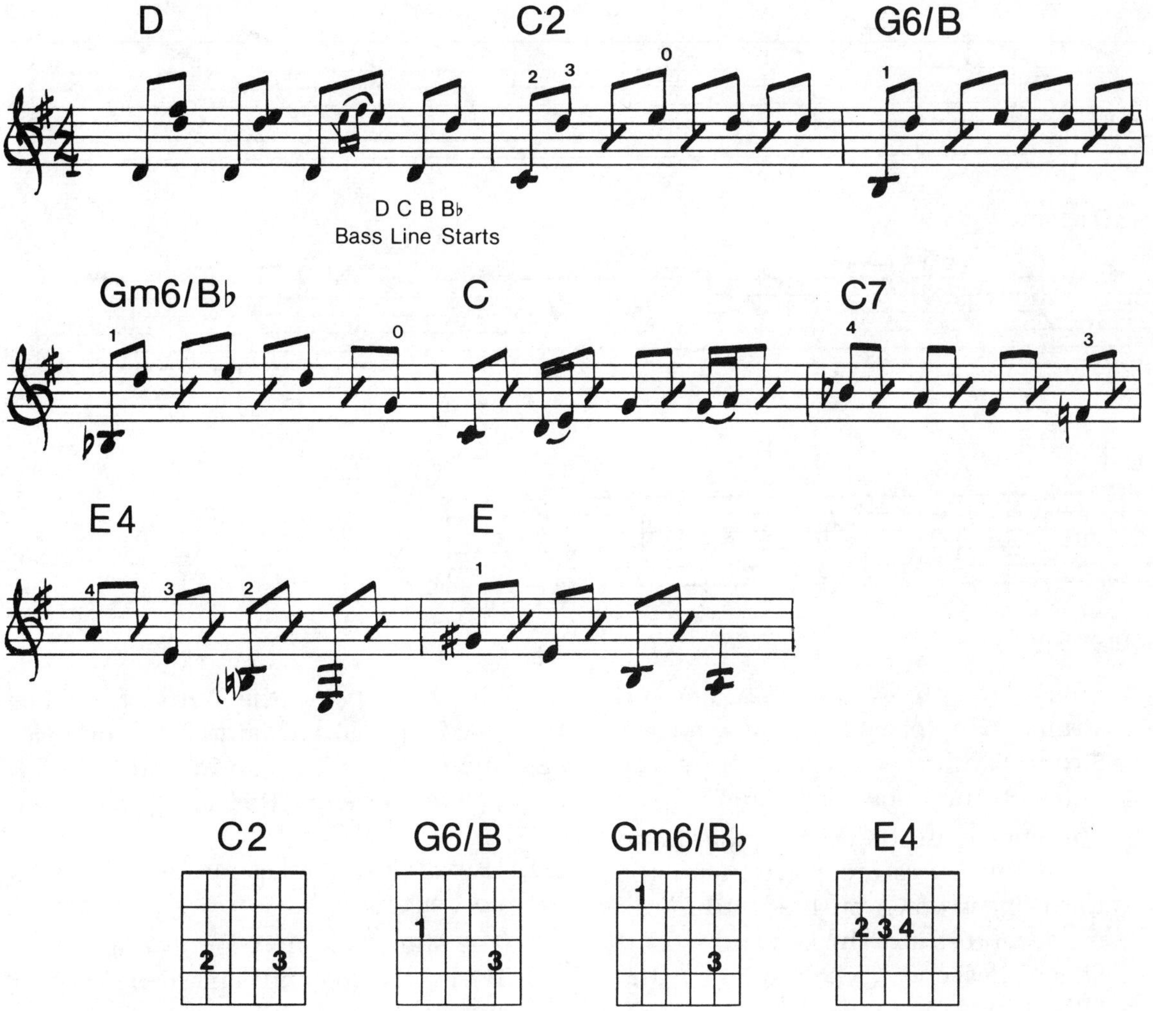

Figure 9-7

Needle and the Damage Done (Tab)

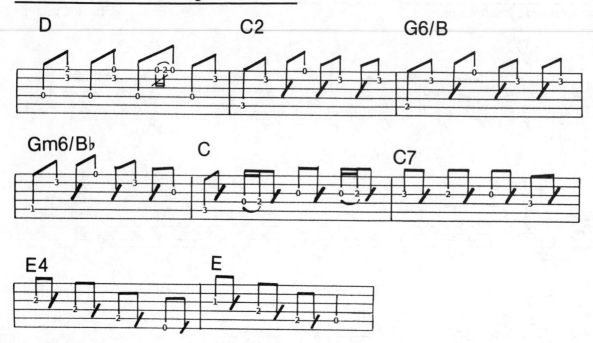

Figure 9-8

notes are played on upbeats and strums are played on downbeats. Strum lightly and accent the single notes on the upbeats.

3. The chords in the second, third, and fourth measures are played with the third finger down on the third fret of the second string. The first and second fingers descend by half steps on the fifth string.

4. The grace note trill in the third beat of measure 1 is a very rapid hammer-on and pull-off played by the second finger on the second fret of the first string.

5. The second half of the introduction is played in a traditional bass and chord style. Strum the chords lightly and emphasize the single notes.

"Yesterday"

In the original recording, Paul McCartney retuned the sixth string a whole step lower to D, an octave below the fourth string. Use the chord grids and tablature notation to locate the bass notes. Keep in mind the following when learning this accompaniment:

1. Use all downstrokes for the bass notes and strums.

2. The short bass line connecting Dm to B♭ in the second line can also be thought of as a bass run.

3. The bass notes in the third line are syncopated.

4. A six-note diatonic descending bass line begins in the middle of the first measure of the chorus.

Diatonic bass lines can be heard in "Dangling Conversation" (Paul Simon), "The Night They Drove Old Dixie Down" (the Band and Joan Baez), "With a Little Help from My Friends" (the Beatles), and "Whiter Shade of Pale" (Procol Harum).

Chromatic bass lines can be heard in "Stairway to Heaven" (Led Zeppelin),

Yesterday (Strumming Patterns with Bass Lines)

as recorded by The Beatles   Words and Music by John Lennon & Paul McCartney

Figure 9-9

Yesterday (Tab)

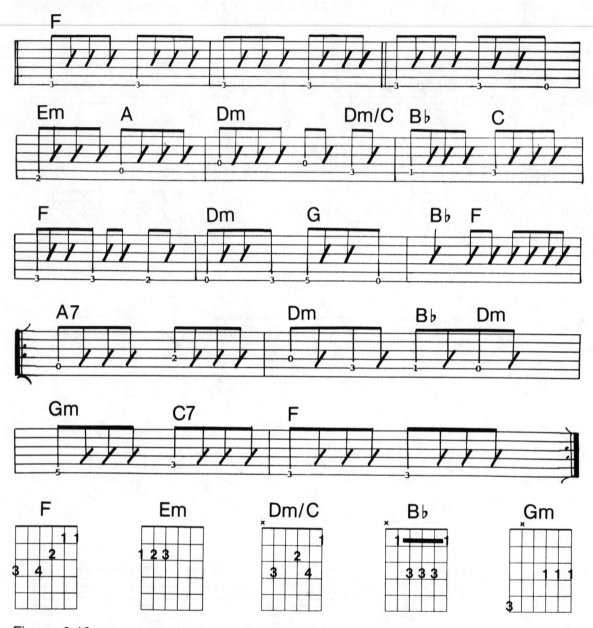

Figure 9-10

"Homeward Bound" (Paul Simon), "Time in a Bottle" (Jim Croce), "If" (David Gates), "Three Times a Lady" (Commodores), "While My Guitar Gently Weeps" (George Harrison), and "Lucy in the Sky with Diamonds" and "Michelle" (the Beatles).

Exercises and Projects

Identify the primary and secondary bass notes, bass runs, and bass lines in "House of the Rising Sun," "Mr. Bojangles," "Needle and the Damage Done," and "Yesterday."

10

MAJOR SCALE INTERVALS AND CHORD CONSTRUCTION

The difference in pitch between notes is called an interval. The study of intervals is a study of sounds. Understanding intervals helps to explain the construction of melodies, chords, progressions, riffs, and improvisations.

This chapter examines intervals with reference to major scales. Each interval is illustrated with melodic fragments from well-known songs. The terminology used here is generally understood by musicians.

Major Scale Intervals

Each note in a major scale implies a unique relationship and sound: the interval from the root of the scale to that note. These major scale intervals are the standards by which all musical intervals are recognized and measured.

Nonscale Notes

Each octave of a major scale contains eight notes. Between the scale degrees are five additional notes. In C major, for example, C♯ or

D♭, D♯ or E♭, F♯ or G♭, G♯ or A♭, and A♯ or B♭ are not on the C scale.

Nonscale notes are identified as alterations of the nearest scale tone. Accidentals are used to identify nonscale notes. For example, E♭ is the flat 3rd and G♯ is the sharp 5th of the C major scale.

Harmonic and Melodic Intervals

Two notes played at the same time form a harmonic interval. Chords are composed of harmonic intervals. Figure 10–1 shows eight harmonic intervals on the C major scale.

Two notes played in sequence form a melodic interval. Figure 10–2 shows melodic intervals on the C major scale. The location of the notes is the same as shown in the tablature of Figure 10–1. Listen to the sound of the harmonic and melodic intervals played on the guitar.

Naming Major Scale Intervals

The scale degree, or number, which identifies the position of a note in the scale

Harmonic Intervals on the C Scale

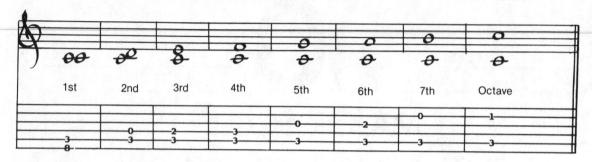

Figure 10-1

Melodic Intervals on the C Scale

Figure 10-2

also identifies the interval formed by that note and the root of the scale.

For example, D is the 2nd degree of the scale, and the interval from C to D is called a 2nd. E is the 3rd degree of the C major scale. The sound of C and E played together is called a 3rd.

Intervals formed by the root and a nonscale tone are named as alterations of the nearest scale tone interval. The interval from C to E♭ is a flat 3rd. The interval formed by C and G♯ is a sharp 5th.

Each major scale interval has a half and whole step equivalent. For example, the interval from C to E, a 3rd on the major scale, measures two whole steps or four half steps. The interval from C to G, a 5th on the major scale, measures seven half steps.

In addition to being numbered, major scale intervals are also given names. The 2nd, 3rd, 6th, and 7th degrees are called major intervals. Major intervals are written with M. For example, C to E is a major 3rd or M3.

The 1st, 4th, 5th and octave are called perfect intervals, written with P. For exam-

ple, the interval from C to G is a perfect 5th or P5.

Intervals defined by nonscale degrees are named as follows:

1. Intervals a half step smaller than major intervals are minor intervals. Minor intervals are written m. The interval from C to E♭ is a minor 3rd, or m3.

2. Intervals a half step smaller than perfect intervals are diminished intervals. Diminished intervals are written dim or D. For example, the interval from C to G♭ is a diminished fifth, or D5.

3. Intervals a half step larger than perfect intervals are augmented intervals. Augmented intervals are written aug or A. The interval from C to G♯ is an augmented fifth, Aug5, or A5.

Figure 10–3 summarizes the names of all the C major intervals and their half step equivalent. Intervals defined on the C major scale are found on all major scales.

Names of Major Scale Intervals

Scale Degree Intervals		
INTERVAL	**HALF-STEPS**	**NAME**
C – C	0	1st, Perfect 1st (P1), Prime or Unison
C – D	2	2nd or Major 2nd (M2)
C – E	4	3rd or M3
C – F	5	4th or Perfect 4th (P4)
C – G	7	5th or P5
C – A	9	6th or M6
C – B	11	7th or M7
C – C	12	8th, P8 or Octave (8ve)

Non-Scale Degree Intervals		
INTERVAL	**HALF-STEPS**	**NAME**
C – D♭	1	♭2nd or minor 2nd (m2)
C – E♭	3	♭3rd or m3
C – F♯	6	♯4th or Augmented 4th (A4)
C – G♭	6	♭5th or Diminished 5th (D5)
C – G♯	8	♯5th or A5
C – A♭	8	♭6th or m6
C – B♭	10	♭7th or m7

Figure 10-3

Names given to intervals are names given to sounds. Figure 10–4 shows the location in first position of twelve different major 3rds. Play the intervals in Figure 10–4 on the guitar. The sound they share is the sound of the interval called a major third. Learn to associate the name of each interval with its particular sound.

Measuring Intervals

To name the interval between two notes, begin with the major scale named by the first note. The scale degree on which the second note falls names the interval between the two notes.

For example, to name the interval from G to E, find E on the G major scale. As shown in Figure 10–5, E is the 6th degree of the G scale. The interval from G to E is an M6 (major 6th). Similarly, the interval formed by G and D is a perfect 5th (P5).

The interval from G to a note not on the G scale is measured with sharps and flats. For example, G to E♭ is a flat 6th or m6. G to D♯ is a sharp 5th or A5.

Major Thirds on Twelve Notes

Figure 10-4

Counting Intervals with Major Scale Degrees

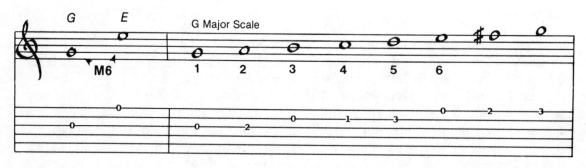

Figure 10-5

Melodic Intervals in Popular Songs

Prime

The interval between a note and itself is called prime or unison. The Beatles' "Help" begins with the same note ten times.

Bob Dylan's "Subterranean Homesick Blues" and "The Times They Are A-Changin'," Antonio Carlos Jobim's "One Note Samba," and Pete Townshend's "I Can See for Miles" are other examples of melodies with repeated notes.

Seconds

The minor 2nd (m2) is a half step. Repeated minor seconds from a chromatic scale, as in the "James Bond Theme" from the movie *Doctor No*.

Help

(Melodic Repetition)   Words and Music by John Lennon & Paul McCartney

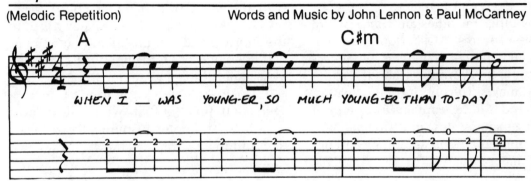

WHEN I __ WAS YOUNG-ER, SO MUCH YOUNG-ER THAN TO-DAY __

Figure 10-6

Copyright ©1965 by Northern Songs Limited. All rights for the United States of America, Mexico, and the Philippines controlled by Maclen Music, Inc., care of ATV Music Corp., 6255 Sunset Blvd., Los Angeles, California 90028. All rights reserved. Used by permission.

The James Bond Theme

(Minor 2nds or Chromatic Scale)   Words and Music by Monty Norman

Figure 10-7

©1962 by United Artists Music Ltd. All rights for the United States of America and Canada controlled by UnartMusic Corp. All rights assigned to CBS Catalogue Partnership. All rights administered by CBS U Catalog. All rights reserved. Used by permission. International copyright secured.

Listen for descending chromatic scale fragments in the opening guitar hook of Led Zeppelin's "Dazed and Confused."

Major scales are formed by a pattern of whole steps (M2) and half steps (m2). The melodies of many songs begin with portions of scales. For example, the melody of "This Land Is Your Land" begins on the root of the G major scale.

The Beatles' "With a Little Help from My Friends" ascends and descends by major and minor seconds on an E major scale. The melody begins on the 3rd degree.

"Give My Regards to Broadway" starts on the 5th degree of C major.

Many other melodies are composed of scales. The Ventures' "Walk, Don't Run" begins with an octave of major and minor seconds forming an A minor scale, the same notes as C major. The chorus of the Beatles' "All You Need Is Love" contains fragments of descending major scales, and "Dueling Banjos" is composed around ascending and descending major scales.

Thirds

Thirds are very common in melodies. Folk and popular songs consist mostly of small intervals, such as 2nds and 3rds with fewer large melodic leaps. "Sentimental Journey" begins with a repeated M3. The line ends with a descending chromatic scale.

Notes separated by M3 and m3 are found in chords. In Figure 10–12, the first three notes of "Michael, Row the Boat Ashore" spell the D major chord.

Listen to Cat Stevens' "Morning Has Broken." The melody, adapted from a traditional hymn, begins with four notes on a C major chord. "The Star Spangled Banner" descends and ascends by 3rds. In Figure 10–13, the notes outline a C major chord.

Paul Simon's "Sound of Silence" begins with the notes of a D minor chord, separated by a minor third and major third. In the fourth measure, the melody continues with the notes of a C major chord, separated by a major third and minor third.

Duke Ellington's "It Don't Mean a Thing (if It Ain't Got that Swing)" also moves by thirds. The notes in the first two measures outline a G minor chord.

Fourths and Fifths

Perfect 4ths and 5ths are dramatic, dynamic, and stirring. The theme from *Star Wars* opens with a 4th and a 5th.

The national anthem of France, "La

This Land is Your Land

(Melodic 2nds or Scale Fragment)

Words and Music by Woody Guthrie

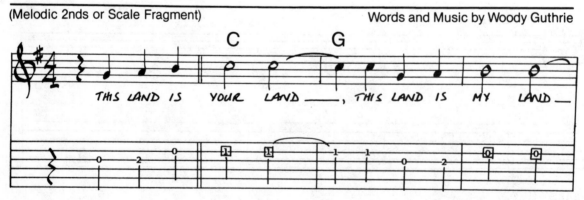

Figure 10-8

With a Little Help from my Friends

(Major and Minor 2nds)   Words and Music by John Lennon & Paul McCartney

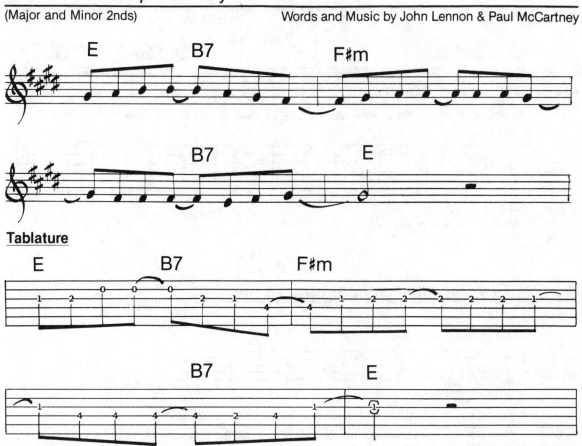

Figure 10-9

Give My Regards to Broadway

(Major and Minor Seconds)   Words and Music by George M. Cohan

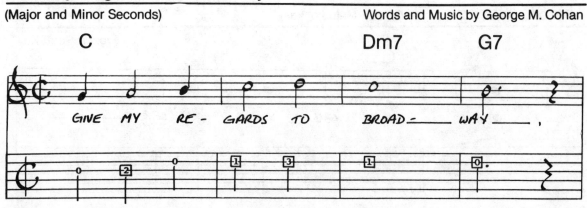

Figure 10-10

Sentimental Journey

(Repeated Major Third)

by Bud Green, Les Brown & Ben Homer

Figure 10-11

Michael, Row the Boat Ashore (Major and Minor 3rds)

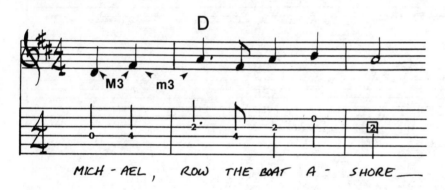

Figure 10-12

The Star-Spangled Banner (Melodic 3rds)

by Francis Scott Key

Figure 10-13

Sound of Silence (Major and Minor 3rds)

Words and Music by Paul Simon

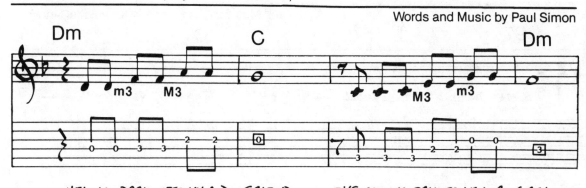

HEL-LO DARK-NESS MY OLD FRIEND — I'VE COME TO TALK TO YOU A-GAIN —.

Figure 10-14

It Don't Mean a Thing (if It Ain't Got that Swing)

(Melodic 3rds in Melody)

by Duke Ellington and Irving Mills

IT   DON'T MEAN A   THING IF   IT   AIN'T GOT THAT SWING

Figure 10-15

Star Wars (Melodic 4th and 5th)

by John Williams

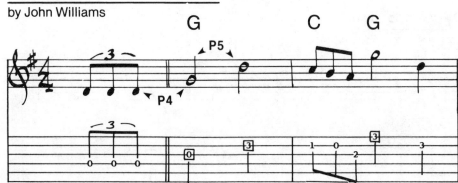

Figure 10-16

I'll Follow the Sun (Melodic Tritone)

Words and Music by John Lennon & Paul McCartney

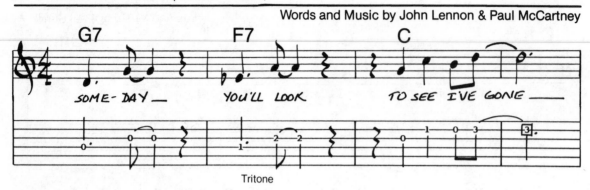

Tritone

Figure 10-17

Marseillaise," is characterized by a perfect 4th between the first two notes. Wagner's traditional "Wedding March," "Here Comes the Bride" also begins with a perfect 4th.

The diminished 5th (D5) and augmented 4th (A4) measure six half steps, or three whole steps. Three whole steps is called a *tritone* (3T). The tritone is a dissonant interval which splits the octave exactly in half. There is a tritone in the second measure of "I'll Follow the Sun" by the Beatles.

Sixths

"Hush, Little Baby" begins with a major 6th.

The first measure of Scott Joplin's "The Entertainer" is filled with repeated minor 6ths. The same interval is also heard in the opening phrase of "Manhã de Carnaval" from the movie *Black Orpheus*.

Other Intervals

Sevenths are rarely heard in popular songs. Errol Garner's jazz classic, "Misty," contains a major 7th in the second measure of the melody. The first line of the Beatles' "Got to Get You into My Life" ends with an ascending minor 7th. The electric guitar introduction to Jimi Hendrix's "Purple Haze" contains several examples of descending minor sevenths. The octave can be heard in the first notes of "Over the Rainbow," sung by Judy Garland.

Hush, Little Baby (Melodic 6th)

Figure 10-18

The Entertainer (Melodic 6th)

Music by Scott Joplin

Figure 10-19

Chord Construction

Chord Spelling, Voicing, Shape, and Fingering

Every chord name specifies a root and a type. In addition, every chord played on the guitar has a spelling, voicing, shape, and fingering. Guitarists should be aware of the four components of every chord they play.

The spelling of a chord is a listing of the unique notes which make up the chord. The voicing of a chord describes the spacing, order, and repetition of those notes which spell the chord. The shape of a chord is the actual pattern formed by the notes on the strings. Most chord shapes can be fingered in more than one way. There is only one way to spell a chord, but many ways to play it on the guitar.

Spelling Chords with Major Scale Intervals

There are several systems for naming the notes of each chord. In this text, all chords are spelled with notes derived from major scales. For example, all C chords—C, Cm, C7, and so on—are spelled with notes derived from the C major scale.

The notes which spell each chord type are determined by a formula. The root of the chord names the major scale on which the chord notes are found. The chord type determines the formula which identifies the scale degrees that are the notes of the chord. Figure 10–20 shows the formulas for the three most common chord types.

Chord Formula Chart

CHORD TYPE	FORMULA	CHORD	SPELLING
Major	1 — 3 — 5	C	C — E — G
minor	1 — ♭3 — 5	Cm	C — E♭ — G
seventh	1 — 3 — 5 — ♭7	C7	C — E — G — B♭

Figure 10-20

Chord Spelling Charts

Use the major scales in Figures 7–1 or 7–6 to fill in the chord spellings of the major, minor, and seventh chords in Figures 10–21 and 10–22. Filled-in charts are found at the end of the chapter in Figures 10–25 and 10–26.

1. The formula for major chords is

R—3—5. R is the root of the scale. The 1st, 3rd and 5th degrees of the C major scale are the notes C—E—G. All voicings of C major chords are spelled with the notes C, E, and G.

Similarly, the G major chord is spelled G—B—D, the root, 3rd and 5th of the G major scale.

2. The formula for minor chords is

MAJOR CHORD SPELLING			
CHORD NAME	ROOT	3	5
C	C	E	G
G			
D			
A			
E			
B			
F#/Gb			
Db			
Ab			
Eb			
Bb			
F			

MINOR CHORD SPELLING			
CHORD NAME	ROOT	b3	5
Cm	C	Eb	G
Gm			
Dm			
Am			
Em			
Bm			
F#m			
Dbm			
Abm			
Ebm			
Bbm			
Fm			

Figure 10-21

R—♭3—5. The 1st, flat 3rd and 5th degrees of the C scale are the notes C—E♭—G.

E minor is spelled E–G–B. The 3rd degree of the E major scale is G♯, the flat 3rd of E is G natural.

3. Major and minor chords are spelled with three notes. The seventh chord is a four-note chord. Seventh chords are spelled with the root, 3rd, 5th and ♭7th of the major scale. R—3—5—♭7 of C are the notes C—E—G—B♭. All C7 chord shapes contain the notes C—E—G—B♭.

The G7 chord is spelled with the R—3—5—♭7 of the G scale, or the notes G—B—D—F. The 7th degree of the G scale is F♯. The flat 7 is F, a half step below F♯.

SEVENTH CHORDS: SPELLING				
CHORD NAME	ROOT	3	5	♭7
C7	C	E	G	B♭
G7				
D7				
A7				
E7				
B7				
F♯7				
D♭7				
A♭7				
E♭7				
B♭7				
F7				

Figure 10-22

Functional Analysis of **E, Em** and **E7**

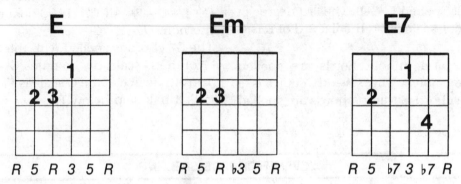

Scale Degrees (Position of Each Note in the E Major Scale)

Figure 10-23

The seventh chord spelled R—3—5—♭7 is also called the *dominant seventh*. The dominant 7th is the most common type of 7th chord. Other types of seventh chords—major 7ths, minor 7ths, and so on—are explained in Chapter 18.

Functional Analysis

The spelling of a chord is a list of the unique notes found in the chord. Analysis is a description of a chord as it is actually played on the guitar. Functional analysis locates each note of a chord on the major scale used to spell the chord and determines which notes are roots, which notes are 3rds, and which notes are 5ths. Functional analysis is also called harmonic analysis.

Figure 10–23 shows the functional or harmonic analysis of E, Em, and E7. The scale degree of each note in the chord is given below the grids. For example, the note on the first string of all E chords is the root of the E major scale. The note on the second string is the 5th degree of the E scale.

Alternate Chord Voicings

Figure 10–24 shows alternate voicings, shapes, and fingerings for first position

Alternate Chord Voicings and Shapes

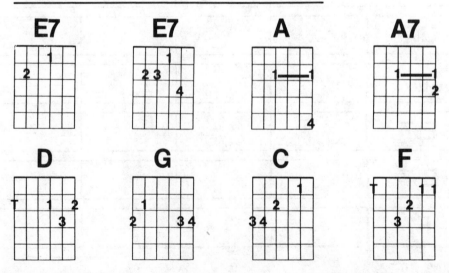

Figure 10-24

chords. These chords have the same spelling but different voicings, shapes, and fingerings from the chords in Chapter 1. The T on the sixth string of the F and D chords represents the left hand thumb. To use the thumb on the sixth string, cradle the guitar neck in the palm of the left hand and reach around the back of the neck with the thumb.

Exercises and Projects

1. Play and memorize the pattern of harmonic or melodic intervals on the C major scale in Figures 10–1 and 10–2.

2. *Consonant* intervals are pleasant, stable, and complete sounding. *Dissonant* intervals sound unstable and incomplete. Each note of the major scale relates to the root with different levels of consonance and dissonance. List the major scale intervals from the most consonant to the most dissonant.

3. Write down or find the sheet music for any melody. Name the intervals between all the notes of the melody.

4. Choose any note. Find the interval from every other note to that note. For example, C is a 4th above G, m7th above D, a m3rd above A, and an augmented 5th above E. Play each interval on the guitar.

5. Memorize the spelling of all major, minor, and seventh chords.

6. Identify the roots, 3rds, 5ths and flat 7ths of the alternate chord voicings in Figure 10–24.

7. Know the spelling and functional anaysis of every chord you play.

MAJOR CHORD SPELLING			
CHORD NAME	ROOT	3	5
C	C	E	G
G	G	B	D
D	D	F#	A
A	A	C#	E
E	E	G#	B
B	B	D#	F#
F#	F#	A#	C#
Db	Db	F	Ab
Ab	Ab	C	Eb
Eb	Eb	G	Bb
Bb	Bb	D	F
F	F	A	C

MINOR CHORD SPELLING			
CHORD NAME	ROOT	b3	5
Cm	C	Eb	G
Gm	G	Bb	D
Dm	D	F	A
Am	A	C	E
Em	E	G	B
Bm	B	D	F#
F#m	F#	A	C#
Dbm	Db	Fb	Ab
Abm	Ab	Cb	Eb
Ebm	Eb	Gb	Bb
Bbm	Bb	Db	F
Fm	F	Ab	C

Figure 10-25

SEVENTH CHORDS: SPELLING			
CHORD NAME	ROOT	3	5	♭7
C7	C	E	G	B♭
G7	G	B	D	F
D7	D	F♯	A	C
A7	A	C♯	E	G
E7	E	G♯	B	D
B7	B	D♯	F♯	A
F♯7	F♯	A♯	C♯	E
D♭7	D♭	F	A♭	C♭
A♭7	A♭	C	E♭	G♭
E♭7	E♭	G	B♭	D♭
B♭7	B♭	D	F	A♭
F7	F	A	C	E♭

Figure 10-26

11

BARRE CHORDS, SIXTEENTH NOTE PATTERNS, AND OPEN TUNINGS

Barre Chords

Barre chords are used in all styles of guitar music. Barre chords are movable shapes that can be played in any position on the fretboard, and they enable the guitarist to play in all keys. These versatile chords are played with the first finger pressing down more than one string. A full barre covers all six strings. A partial barre covers two to five strings.

In chord grid diagrams, a full barre is indicated by a thick horizontal line between a 1 on the first string line and a 1 on the sixth string line. The first finger covers the first and sixth strings, and all the strings in between, as in the illustrations in Figure 1–6.

Thousands of different chords can be played on the guitar. One way of understanding and organizing chord vocabulary is by looking at families of chord shapes. This section is a study of two families of chord shapes: the root sixth string barre chords and the root fifth string barre chords.

Root Sixth String Barre Chords

The roots of E, Em, and E7 are on the open sixth string. These three chords are root sixth string chord shapes. All the chords in Figure 11–1 are root sixth string chord shapes. When the chord shapes are played with open strings, as in the top row, the note on the sixth string is E, and the chords are simply E, Em, and E7. Scale degrees below the grids indicate the harmonic function of each note in the chord.

Move the root sixth string chord shapes up a fret and place a full barre on the first fret. Use second, third, and fourth fingers to form chord shapes above the barre. The note on the sixth string is F and the chords are F major, Fm, and F7, as in the second row of chords.

In the bottom row, root sixth string chord shapes are played above a full barre at the second fret. The note on the second fret of the sixth string is F♯, and the chords are F♯, F♯m, and F♯7.

Any major, minor, or seventh chord can be played with a root sixth string barre chord shape. Locate the root of the chord

Root Sixth String Barre Chord Shapes

NOTES ON THE SIXTH STRING		ROOT ⑥ Major Shape	ROOT ⑥ Minor Shape	ROOT ⑥ Seventh Shape
FRET	NOTE			
Open	E	**E**	**Em**	**E7**
I	F			
II	F#/G♭			
III	G	R 5 R 3 5 R	R 5 R♭3 5 R	R 5 ♭7 3 ♭7 R
IV	G#/A♭	**F**	**Fm**	**F7**
V	A			
VI	A#/B♭			
VII	B	R 5 R 3 5 R	R 5 R♭3 5 R	R 5 ♭7 3 ♭7 R
VIII	C	**F#**	**F#m**	**F#7**
IX	C#/D♭			
X	D			
XI	D#/E♭	R 5 R 3 5 R	R 5 R♭3 5 R	R 5 ♭7 3 ♭7 R
XII	E			

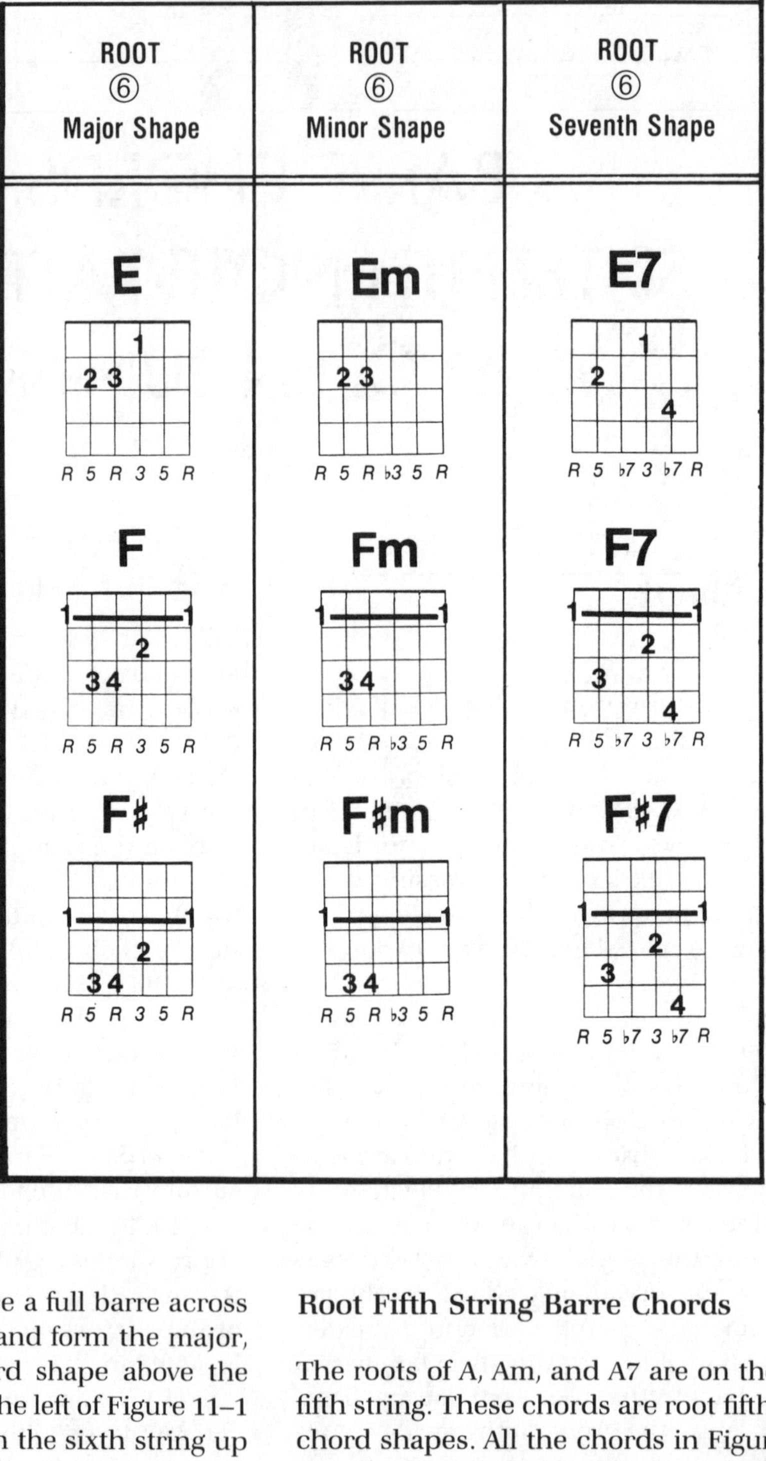

Figure 11-1

on the sixth string, place a full barre across the strings at that fret, and form the major, minor, or seventh chord shape above the barre. The columns on the left of Figure 11–1 show names of notes on the sixth string up to the twelfth fret.

Root Fifth String Barre Chords

The roots of A, Am, and A7 are on the open fifth string. These chords are root fifth string chord shapes. All the chords in Figure 11–2 are root fifth string chord shapes. When the

Root Fifth String Barre Chord Shapes

NOTES ON THE FIFTH STRING		ROOT ⑤ Major Shape	ROOT ⑤ Minor Shape	ROOT ⑤ Seventh Shape
FRET	NOTE			
Open	A			
I	A#/Bb	**A**	**Am**	**A7**
II	B			
III	C			
IV	C#/Db	**Bb**	**Bbm**	**Bb7**
V	D			
VI	D#/Eb			
VII	E			
VIII	F	**B**	**Bm**	**B7**
IX	F#/Gb			
X	G			
XI	G#/Ab			
XII	A			

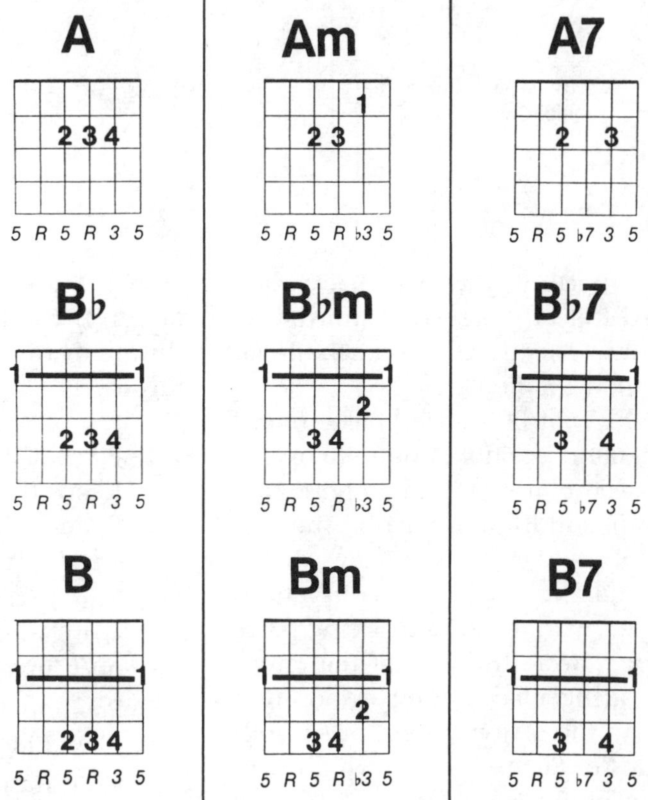

Figure 11-2

chord shapes are played with open strings, as in the top row, the note on the fifth string is A, and the chords are simply A, Am, and A7.

The middle row of Figure 11–2 shows these same chord shapes with the first finger placed across all six strings at the first fret. The name of the note on the fifth string covered by the barre at the first fret is A# or Bb. Traditionally, the chords are named as Bb, Bbm, and Bb7.

An alternate fingering for Bb major uses

Two Ways to Play C minor with Barre Chords

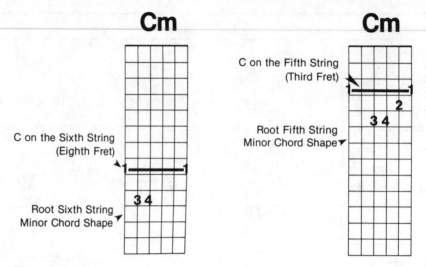

Figure 11-3

the third or fourth fingers bent backwards on the third fret of the second, third, and fourth strings. The third or fourth finger does not touch the first string.

Move the root fifth string barre chord shapes to second position. The note on the fifth string second fret is B. The chords are named B, Bm, and B7, as shown in the bottom row.

Any major, minor, or seventh chord can be played with a root fifth string barre chord shape. Locate the root of the chord on the fifth string, place a full barre on that fret, and form the major, minor, or seventh chord shapes of Figure 11–2 above the bar. The columns on the left of Figure 11–2 show the location of note names up to the twelfth fret of the fifth string.

Any major, minor, or seventh chord can be played in two positions: with a root sixth string chord shape, and with a root fifth string chord shape. Figure 11–3 shows how two barre chord shapes are used to play Cm.

Barre Chord Exercise

If you have trouble playing barre chords at the first fret, practice at the fifth fret or higher. Move down one fret at a time to the first fret. The following routine will develop the ability to press each string equally with a full barre:

1. Place a full barre down on any fret. Keep the second, third, and fourth fingers above the strings, pointing towards the frets.
2. The first finger holds down all six strings by itself. Do not place the second finger on top of the first finger.
3. Position the first finger until you can play a clear note on the sixth string.
4. Do not move the barre. Play the strings one at a time. Make each string ring clearly in its turn. Feel how the first finger can push down each string while laying across all six.
5. Repeat from the sixth string as many times as necessary.

Using Barre Chords

Figure 11–4a is a common progression in A♭. Roman numerals below the staff indicate positions. IV in the first two measures indicates a barre at the fourth fret.

A Common Progression in A♭ Using Barre Chords

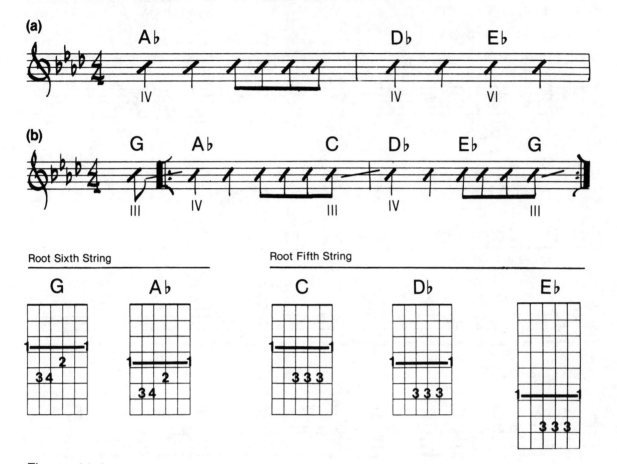

Figure 11-4

The variation in Figure 11–4b is created by approaching each chord with a slide from one fret below. The introduction to Linda Ronstadt's recording of "When Will I be Loved?" is an example of a sliding barre chord shape.

Figure 11–5 shows the chord progression used in "Midnight Hour." The chords are played with all root sixth string barre chords. Roman numerals below the staff indicate at which frets to place the barre.

Jim Croce used the accompaniment in Figure 11–6 for "Bad, Bad, Leroy Brown." In this accompaniment, barre chords change on every beat.

Keep in mind the following when learning this guitar part:

1. The first measure and a half is an alternation between barre chords G and C. Both chords are played in third position, as indicated by the roman numeral III below the staff.

2. The third and fourth beats of the second measure show a chromatically ascending barre chord.

3. The first two measures are repeated a whole step higher.

4. The chords change more frequently beginning in the fifth measure and again in the seventh measure.

5. D7 is a first position C7 chord shape moved up two frets. Change to D7 on the first upbeat of the last measure.

Midnight Hour (Progression with Barre Chords)

as recorded by Wilson Pickett   by Wilson Pickett & Steve Cropper

Use All Root Sixth String Shape

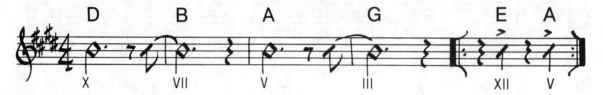

Figure 11-5

Bad, Bad, Leroy Brown (Progression with Barre Chords)

as recorded by Jim Croce   by Jim Croce

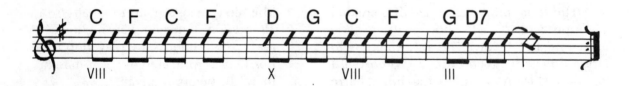

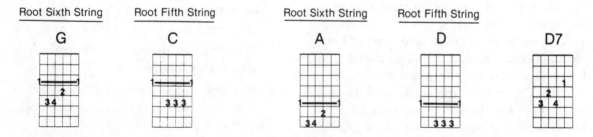

Root Sixth String   Root Fifth String   Root Sixth String   Root Fifth String

G   C   A   D   D7

Figure 11-6

Cycle of Fourths

The chord progression in Figure 11–7 is called the *cycle of fourths*. The interval between the chords is always a 4th. A chord change on the cycle of fourths is common in many styles of music. Roman numerals indicate fret positions. For example, the first C is played with a full barre at the eighth fret. The progression is played with:

a. All root sixth string barre chord shapes.
b. All root fifth string barre chord shapes.
c. Alternating between root sixth and root fifth string shapes.

Chord Progression: Cycle of Fourths

Figure 11-7

Sixteenth Note Strumming Patterns

Sixteenth note strums are played twice as fast as eighth notes strums. At slow tempos, a few sixteenth note strums added to a pattern can have an interesting effect. Keith Richards used the pattern in Figure 11–8 in "Wild Horses," recorded by the Rolling Stones.

Pete Townshend used the patterns in Figure 11–9 in "Pinball Wizard." All the eighth notes in Figure 11–9 are played with downstrokes. The sixteenth note strums are played with rapidly alternating down- and upstrokes. Strum everything lightly except the accents, which are played with great emphasis. The Bsus4 chord is explained in Chapter 18.

The sixteenth notes at the end of the first measure of 11–9b are played on an upbeat. The pattern of upbeat sixteenth notes followed by a quarter note is also heard in "Wild Horses" (Figure 11–8), "Jumping Jack Flash" (Figure 11–12), and at the end of "Brown Sugar" (Figure 18–7).

Figure 11–10 shows a popular rhythm. The essence of this style is in the contrast of rhythms created by the left and right hands. The right hand plays up and down sixteenth notes across muted strings. Mute the strings by keeping the chord shape in place and releasing tension in the left hand so that the fingers do not push the strings against the frets. Muted strums are indicated by an x in place of a strum symbol.

The left hand squeezes a chord shape against the fretboard on selected parts of the down- and upbeats, indicated by diagonal strum symbols. The patterns in Figure 11–10 can be played with any full barre chord shape.

Figure 11–10a is four beats of muted strings only. Figure 11–10b is a modern rhythm guitar cliché. Play the pattern as follows:

1. Squeeze the chord against the frets only when a strum symbol appears in the rhythm. The right hand plays sixteenth notes independently of whether the left hand mutes or plays a chord shape.

Wild Horses (Sixteenth Note Strumming Pattern)

as recorded by The Rolling Stones   Words and Music by Mick Jagger and Keith Richards

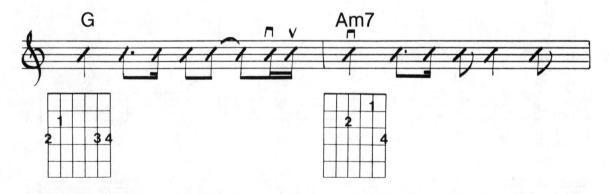

Figure 11-8

Pinball Wizard

as recorded by Pete Townshend

Words and Music by Pete Townshend

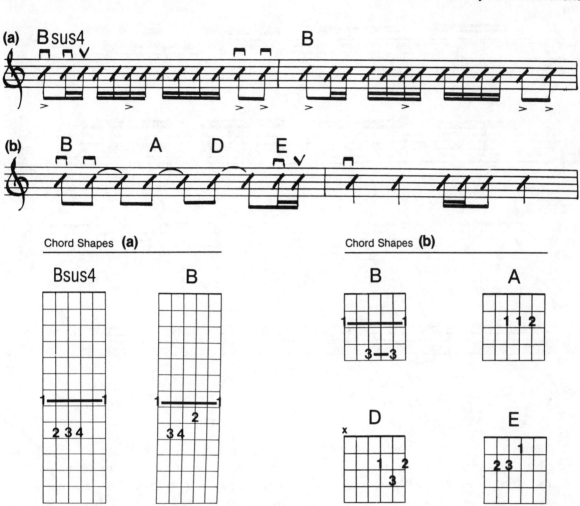

Figure 11-9

Sixteenth Note Strumming Pattern: Mute and Squeeze

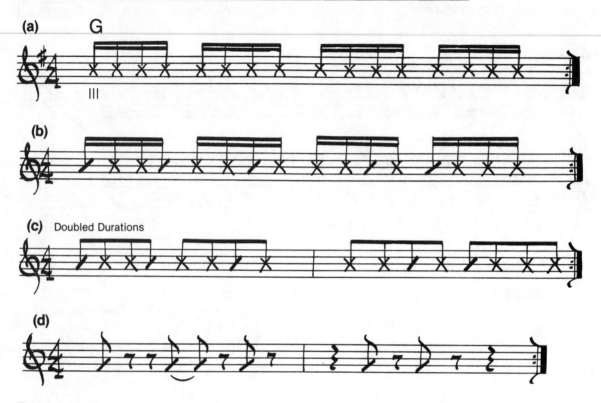

Figure 11-10

2. Figure 11–10c is the same rhythm with time values doubled. Figure 11–10d is the rhythm written with rests.

3. The mute and squeeze sixteenth note pattern is often heard with ninths and minor sevenths, especially played on the treble strings in the higher positions (see Chapter 18: Chord Vocabulary).

Open Tunings

Other guitar tunings are possible in addition to E–A–D–G–B–E. When the guitar is tuned to open A, the six open strings sound an A major chord. When the guitar is tuned to open G, the unfretted strings sound a G chord. Figure 11–11 shows traditional tunings for open A and open G.

Open A and open G are essentially the same. The function of the notes on the strings are identical. To change from standard tuning to open A, three strings are raised a whole step, as if fingering an A major chord. To change from standard to open G, three different strings are dropped a whole step.

The open tuning examples are in the key of B. Use open G tuning and a capo at the fourth fret or open A tuning and a capo at the second fret.

"Jumping Jack Flash"

Figure 11–12 shows rhythm guitar parts used by Keith Richards in the Rolling Stones' recording. The open tuning allows the guitarist to play power chord shapes with only one finger.

Open Tunings

			OPEN TUNING: Root⑤		
String	OPEN G Tuning	Retune As Below	STANDARD Tuning	Retune As Below	OPEN A Tuning
⑥	D	◄ down a whole step	E		E
⑤	G	◄ down a whole step	A		A
④	D		D	up a whole step ►	E
③	G		G	up a whole step ►	A
②	B		B	up a whole step ►	C♯
①	D	◄ down a whole step	E		E

Figure 11-11

Jumping Jack Flash (Open Tuning)

as recorded by The Rolling Stones   Words and Music by Mick Jagger and Keith Richards

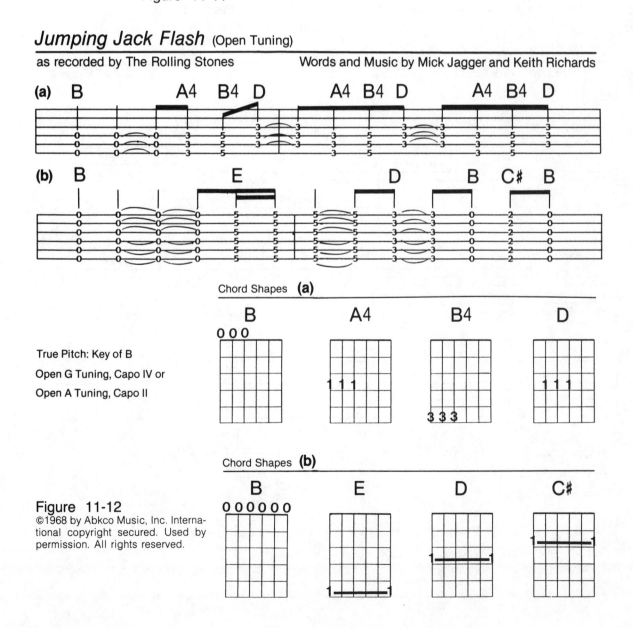

True Pitch: Key of B

Open G Tuning, Capo IV or

Open A Tuning, Capo II

Figure 11-12

All chord shapes in 11–12a are played with partial barre chords on the bass strings, except B, which is played on open strings. Use all downstrokes. All except the first chord in 12b are played with full barres. Play the sixteenth notes with light down- and upstrokes. Accent the following downbeat.

"Circle Game"

Joni Mitchell used an open tuning in "Circle Game" to create unusual voicings, complexity, and clarity. Figure 11–13 shows the fingerpicking patterns and chord shapes used in the recording.

The introduction begins at *a*. The vo-cals begin at *b*. The right hand thumb picks all the notes on the fifth and fourth strings.

Exercises and Projects

1. Memorize the names of all the notes on the sixth and fifth strings.

2. Play the cycle of fourths chord progression with minor or seventh chords. Use any one measure strumming or picking pattern, including the sixteenth note mute and squeeze rhythm.

3. The notes of Figure 11–12a ("Jumping Jack Flash") can be played above a full barre at the seventh fret in standard tuning. Find the chord shapes.

Circle Game (Open Tuning)

as recorded by Joni Mitchell

by Joni Mitchell

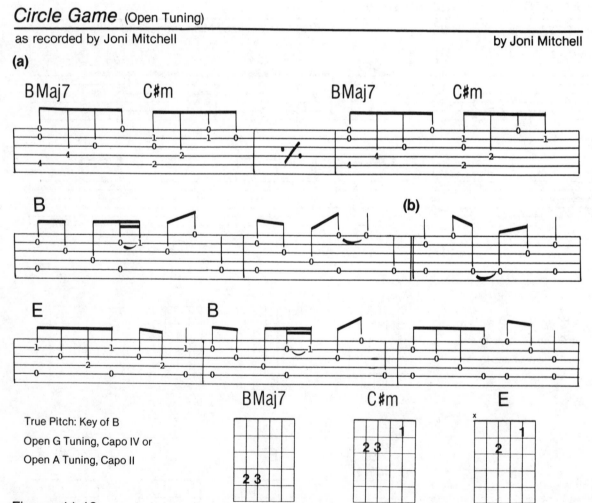

Figure 11-13

True Pitch: Key of B

Open G Tuning, Capo IV or

Open A Tuning, Capo II

12

ROCK SHUFFLE PATTERNS
AND CHROMATIC OCTAVES

Rock and Roll Shuffle

The shuffle rhythm has its origin in blues guitar. The shuffle has been used throughout the evolution of rock and roll and electric guitar music. It has become an integral part of popular American music styles including country and western and gospel music. The patterns in this chapter are found in the transcriptions in Chapter 17.

Figure 12–1 shows a shuffle in E.

Keep in mind the following when playing the shuffle in E:

1. The first finger stays down on the second fret of the fifth string throughout the pattern.
2. The third finger reaches all the way to the fourth fret of the fifth string on the second and fourth beats.

Shuffle in E

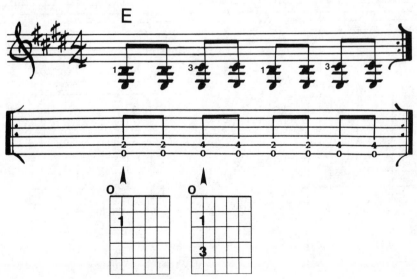

Figure 12-1

3. Brush the sixth and fifth strings together with a pick or with the right hand thumb. Make a percussive, swift sound.

4. The second and fourth beats are accented.

The fingering used for the E shuffle moves to the fifth and fourth strings for the shuffle in A. The shuffle in E and the shuffle in A are fingered the same, but on different strings.

Figure 12–2a shows one measure each of the shuffle in E and A. The shuffle in D is played on the fourth and third strings. Figure 12–2b shows the shuffle in A and D.

The Twelve Bar Blues

The twelve bar blues is a commonly used song structure in popular music. The twelve bar blues is traditionally divided into three lines of four measures each, as in Figure

Shuffle in E and A, Shuffle in A and D

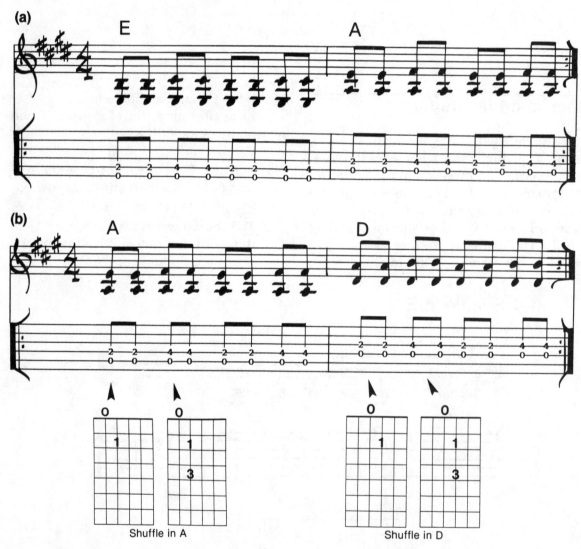

Figure 12-2

12–3. Each measure is played as four beats of the shuffle pattern. The variations in Figure 12–4 can be applied to D and E patterns.

The following rock and roll songs are constructed around the twelve bar blues progression and its variations. Many of these songs were also recorded with shuffle patterns: "Johnny B. Goode," "Roll Over, Beethoven," "Memphis," and "Around and Around" (Chuck Berry); "Oh Boy" and "Rave On" (Buddy Holly); "Hound Dog" and "Blue Suede Shoes" (Elvis Presley); and "Rock Around the Clock," (Bill Haley and the Comets).

Twelve bar blues progressions are found in these rhythm and blues songs:

Twelve Bar Blues in A

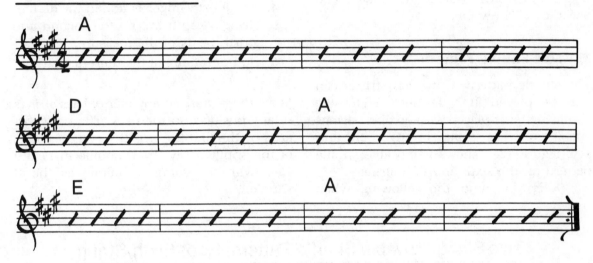

Figure 12-3

Figure 12-4

Shuffle Pattern Variations

"Can I Get a Witness" (Marvin Gaye); "Green Onions" (Booker T. and the M.G.'s); "Mustang Sally" (Wilson Pickett); "The Way You Do the Things You Do" (The Temptations); and "Papa's Got a Brand New Bag" (James Brown).

Other titles characterized by the twelve bar blues progression include: "Birthday," "I'm Down," "Can't Buy Me Love," and "Ballad of John and Yoko" (the Beatles); "Blame It on Cain" (Elvis Costello); and "Sexy and Seventeen" (Stray Cats).

Movable Shuffle Patterns

The shuffle pattern with open strings can only be played in A, D, and E. Movable shuffle patterns played with no open strings enable guitarists to play in any chord and key. Figure 12–5 shows a movable shuffle pattern on the sixth and fifth strings.

Keep in mind the following when playing the movable shuffle:

1. The pattern is named by the note under the first finger. In Figure 12–5, the first finger is on sixth string, third fret G.
2. The first finger does not form a barre.
3. The first and third fingers stay down throughout the movable shuffle pattern.
4. The fourth finger is added to the fifth string seventh fret on the second and fourth beats of the measure.
5. Do not hit any of the unfretted strings.

Move the pattern to any pair of bass strings in any position on the neck. The note covered by the first finger is the root, or name, of the shuffle. Play the C shuffle in Figure 12–6 with the same technique as the G shuffle.

Two-String Movable Shuffle Pattern, Root Sixth String

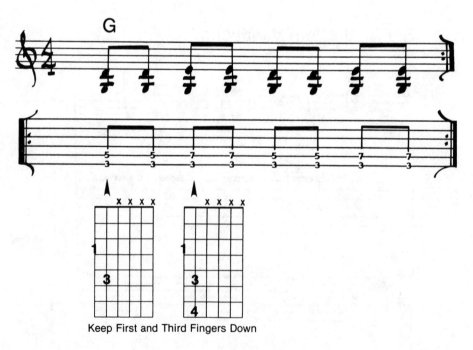

Keep First and Third Fingers Down

Figure 12-5

Two-String Movable Shuffle Pattern, Root Fifth String

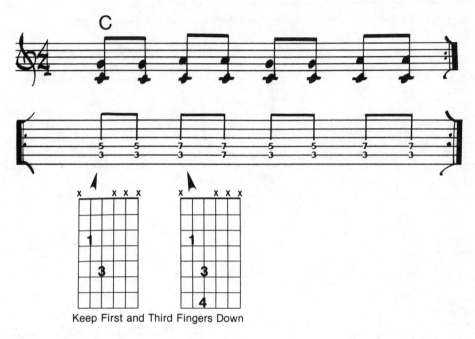

Keep First and Third Fingers Down

Figure 12-6

Chromatic Scale in Octaves in First Position

Playing barre chords and movable shuffle patterns requires the use of the fourth finger. Practicing the chromatic scale in octaves in first position strengthens and coordinates all four left hand fingers.

Keep in mind the following when practicing the chromatic octaves:

1. Start with the open sixth string and the E one octave higher on the fourth string, second fret. Play the notes together.
2. Raise both E notes one fret to F on the first fret of the sixth string and third fret of the fourth string.
3. Continue to raise both notes a half step, or one fret.
4. Play in first position: your first finger on the first fret, second finger on the sec-

ond fret, third finger on the third fret, and fourth finger on the fourth fret only. Use open strings if necessary.
5. Let each pair of notes ring for as long as possible.
6. Name the notes as you play them.

Right Hand Variations

Figure 12–9 shows right hand variations for the chromatic octave exercise. Right hand fingers are indicated in staff notation in measures a–d. Measure e shows the location of the notes in tablature. Apply each variation to the entire ascending and descending first position chromatic scale in octaves.

The chromatic octaves can also be played with a flatpick by staggering the notes—bass, treble, bass, treble. Hold the fingers on their frets so that the low and high notes blend into each other. Use all downstrokes or alternate down- and upstrokes.

Chromatic Scale in Octaves in First Position

Numbers in Circles are Strings   Small Numbers Next to Notes are Left Hand Fingers and Frets

Figure 12-7

Chromatic Scale in Octaves (Tab)

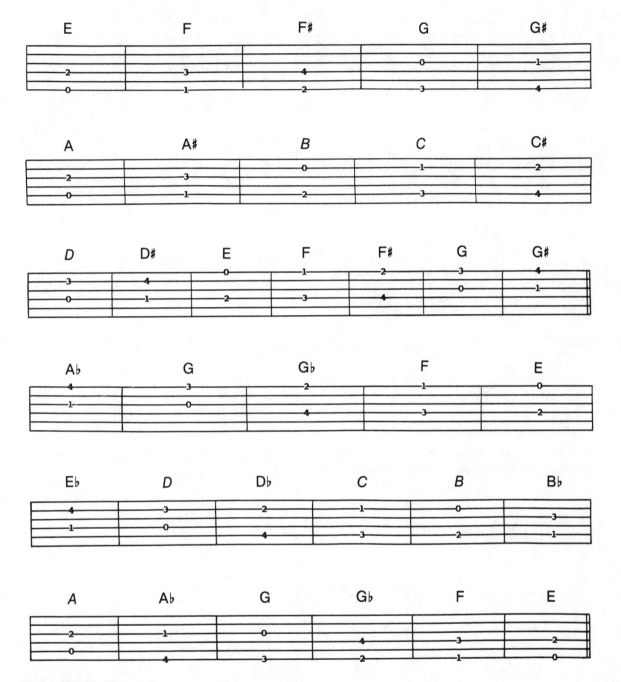

Play in First Position:
  1st Finger Plays 1st Fret,   2nd Finger Plays 2nd Fret,   3rd Finger Plays 3rd Fret,   4th Finger Plays 4th Fret.

Figure 12-8

Chromatic Octaves, Right Hand Variations

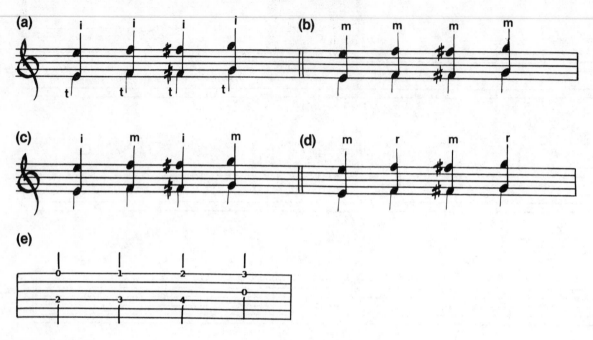

Figure 12-9

Exercises and Projects

1. Memorize the twelve bar blues in A.
2. Play the twelve bar blues in A using movable two-string shuffle patterns.
3. Play one measure of movable shuffle pattern for each chord on the cycle of fourths progression in Figure 11–7.
4. Memorize the chromatic scale in octaves in first position.

13

TRANSPOSING AND COMMON CHORD PROGRESSIONS

Changing a song from one key to another is called *transposing.* A song is transposed when you know it in one key and want to play in another, when you have the sheet music to a song and the chords are in a difficult key, or when the music is written in a different key from the recording.

Transposing Chord Progressions

There are two approaches to transposing chord progressions:

1. Raise or lower every chord by an equal interval. Transposing with this method requires a knowledge of intervals between notes.
2. Preserve the relationships between the chords. Transposing with this method requires a knowledge of the major scales.

Transposing by Changing Each Chord

Figure 13–1a shows a progression in the key of B♭.

Transpose to the key of C using inter-vals as follows:

1. Find the interval from B♭ to C. B♭ to C is a whole step.
2. Raise the other chords in the progression by the same interval. A whole step above E♭ is F, as in Figure 13–1b.

Transpose the progression so that the first chord is E, as follows:

1. Find the interval from B♭ to E. B♭ to E is six half steps, three whole steps, or a tritone.
2. Raise the other chords by the same interval. Three whole steps above E♭ is A, as in Figure 13–1c.

Preserve chord types. If the chords in Figure 13–1 were B♭m7 and E♭7, the transposed progressions are Cm7 and F7, or Em7 and A7.

Transposing by Preserving Relationships

The relationships between the chords of a progression are expressed in terms of major

A Simple Chord Progression in B♭, C and E

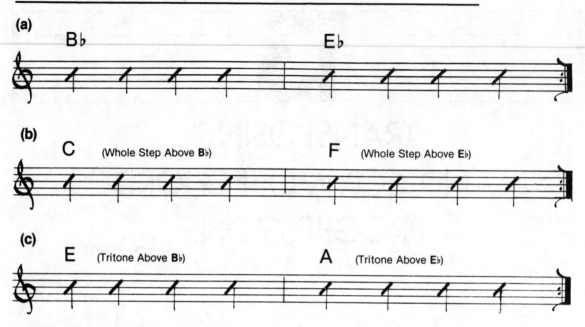

Figure 13-1

scale degrees. Transpose a chord progression using scale degrees as follows:

1. Locate the roots of the chords on the major scale of the key of the progression. B♭ is the 1st degree and E♭ is the 4th degree of the B♭ scale.

2. Rewrite the chord with roman numerals corresponding to the scale degrees of the chord roots. The progression B♭—E♭ is I—IV in the key of B♭.

3. The notes on other scales which correspond to the roman numerals are the roots of the transposed progression.

   On the C major scale, the 1st degree is C and the 4th degree is F. I—IV is C and F major. The 1st and 4th degrees of the E major scale are E and A. I—IV in the key of E are the chords E and A.

4. Chord types are written after roman numerals. Cm—F7 in the key of C is Im—IV7. Roman numerals alone are major chords.

5. Chords whose roots do not fall on major scale notes are expressed as alterations of the nearest scale degree. For

example, G and F form a I—♭VII progression. F is the ♭7 degree of the G scale.

Typical Progressions in Contemporary Songs

The short progressions in this section are found in many different styles of music. Learning to recognize the progressions by ear and in written music makes transcribing and transposing easier. Each chord sequence is shown with quarter note strums. In actual practice, many different rhythm patterns are used. Chords for one key are shown below the staff for each progression.

Chord Types and Scale Degrees

Chord types are often associated with particular scale degrees. For example, the I, IV, and V are usually major chords. Chords built on the 2nd, 3rd, and 6th degrees are minors: IIm, IIIm and VIm. The simple I—IV progression is heard in "Imagine" (John Lennon), "You Can't Always Get What You Want" (Rolling Stones), "96 Tears" (? and the

Mysterians), "For What It's Worth" (Steven Stills), and "Do You Believe in Magic?" (John Sebastian).

Figure 13–2 shows some progressions with I—IV—V. Rock and roll songs whose chord progressions are combinations of I—IV—V major chords include "Wild Thing," "Crimson and Clover," "Good Lovin'," "Summertime Blues," and "Louie, Louie."

Typical Progressions with Minor Chords

The VIm is closely related to the I major. "Maybe Baby" (Buddy Holly), "Mrs. Robinson" (Paul Simon), "New Kid in Town" (Eagles), and "Miracle Man" (Elvis Costello) use I—VIm throughout.

Figure 13–3 shows variations of I—VIm—IIm—V progressions. Popular

Typical **I IV V** Progressions

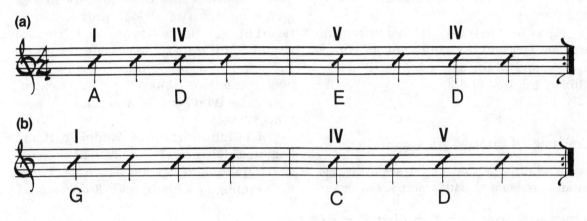

Figure 13-2

I VIm IIm V, and Variations

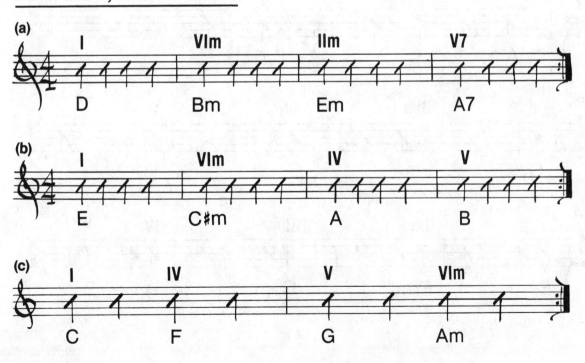

Figure 13-3

songs which use these progressions include "Stand by Me" and "You Send Me" (Sam Cooke), "All My Lovin'," "A Day in the Life," and "Penny Lane" (the Beatles), "Crocodile Rock" (Elton John), "Hungry Heart" (Bruce Springsteen), and "Every Breath You Take" (The Police).

Examples of songs with the IIIm chord shown in Figure 13–4 include "Watching the Detectives" (Elvis Costello), "The Weight" (The Band), "All Along the Watchtower" and "I Shall be Released" (Bob Dylan), "Crazy on You" (Heart), "Here, There, and Everywhere" (the Beatles).

"We Are the World" (Lionel Richie and Michael Jackson) uses all the major chords (I, IV, V) and all the minor chords (IIm, IIIm, VIm) of the Key of E.

Unexpected Chord Types

Major chords can occur on scale degrees usually associated with minors. For exam-ple, the 2nd degree chord is usually minor. The unexpected II major is used in "Heatwave" (Martha and the Vandellas), "Sgt. Pepper's Lonely Hearts Club Band" (the Beatles), and "Welcome to the Working Week" (Elvis Costello).

The I—III—IV (all majors) progression is used in "Dock of the Bay" (Otis Redding) and "Seeds and Stems" (Commander Cody).

NonScale Degree Chord Roots

The ♭III and ♭VII chords are common in rock guitar music. The I—♭VII progression is heard in "You Really Got Me" and "Tired of Waiting" (the Kinks), "Willy and the Hand Jive" and "Cocaine" (Eric Clapton), "Psy-chotic Reaction" (Count Five), "My Genera-tion" (The Who), and "I Want Candy" (Bow Wow Wow).

The introduction to "Midnight Hour" (Figure 11–5) is a ♭VII—V—IV—♭III progres-sion. The ♭III and ♭VII chords are also heard in "Jumping Jack Flash" and "Brown Sugar"

Progressions with the IIIm Chord

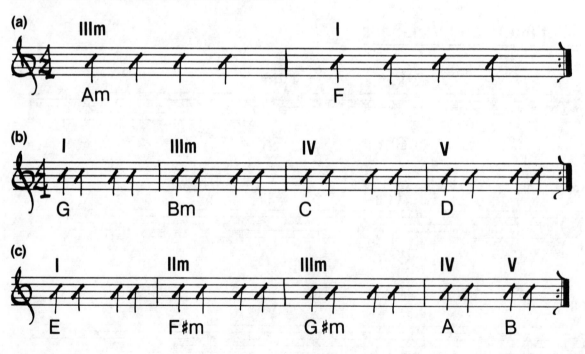

Figure 13-4

(the Rolling Stones), "Communication Breakdown" (Led Zeppelin), "Purple Haze" (Jimi Hendrix), "Green Onions" (Booker T. and the M.G.'s), and "Gloria" (Van Morrison).

The progression in Figure 13–6 is heard in Spanish flamenco music. It is also the progression in "Hit the Road, Jack" (Ray Charles), "Walk, Don't Run" (the Ventures), and "Stray Cat Strut" (Stray Cats).

Transposing Riffs and Melodies

If you like the sound of a riff played around one chord, transposing will allow you to play the same riff with every other chord. Transpose as follows:

1. Use the major scale with the same root name as the chord against which the

Typical Progressions with ♭III and ♭VII

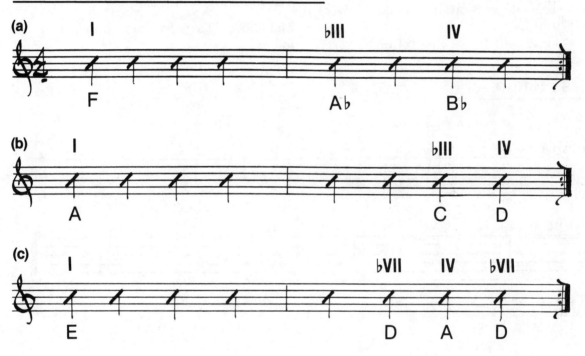

Figure 13-5

The "Flamenco" Progression: IVm ♭III ♭II I

Figure 13-6

riff is played. Find the scale degree of each note in the riff.

2. The same sequence of scale degrees on other major scales will produce the sound of the riff.

3. Preserve the timing of the notes.

The numbers above the notes in Figure 13–7 are scale degrees. The first four notes are the root, 3rd, 5th, and 6th degrees of the A major scale.

To transpose to the key of E, play the same scale degrees on the E major scale, as in Figure 13–8.

Songs which use this riff or its varia-tions include "Hot Rod Lincoln" (Commander Cody), "Let There be Rock" (AC/DC), "Rock This Town" (Stray Cats), "Jailhouse Rock" and "Hound Dog" (Elvis Presley), "My Girl" (Smokey Robinson), "Chuck E.'s in Love" (Rickie Lee Jones), "Birthday" and "Day Tripper" (the Beatles), and "Neutron Dance" (Pointer Sisters).

Figure 13–9 shows some variations on the bass riff.

Transposing Melodies

Melodies, like riffs, are transposed as follows:

Bass Riff in A

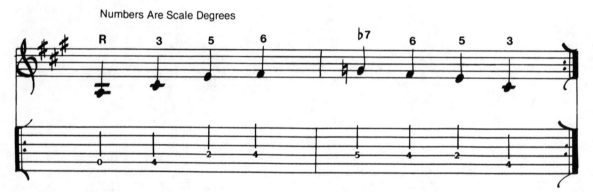

Figure 13-7

Bass Riff Transposed to E

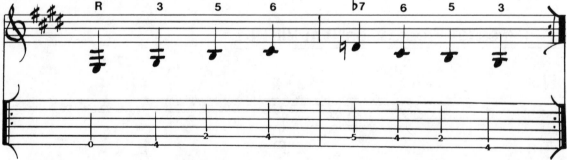

Figure 13-8

Bass Riff Variations

Figure 13-9

1. Find the scale degree of every note in the melody.
2. Find the sequence of scale degrees in other major scales.
3. Preserve the duration of each note.
4. Transpose the accompanying chords.

Exercises and Projects

1. Transpose the twelve bar blues progression to all twelve keys.

2. Transpose any riff to all keys.
3. Transpose the typical progressions in this chapter to all keys.
4. Learn a favorite song by ear or by reading the sheet music. Transpose the melody and chord progression to all twelve keys.
5. Find the short progressions discussed in this chapter in the chord progressions of other songs.

14

SINGLE NOTE STYLES: SCALES

Rhythm guitarists are skilled in playing chords; lead guitarists are skilled in playing scales. The rhythm guitarist strums chords in time with the bass and drums. The lead guitarist plays short melodic phrases called hooks, riffs, or fills, or instrumental solos.

Practicing Scales

The study of scales and scale patterns should supplement a repertoire of song melodies, authentic riffs, transcribed solos, and creative imagination. The more melodies and solos you can play, the more meaningful and useful the study of scale patterns becomes. This chapter focuses on commonly used pentatonic and major scale patterns. The scale patterns introduced in this chapter are used in all styles of lead guitar playing.

Pentatonic Scales

Pentatonic scales are each made up of five different notes. The major pentatonic and minor pentatonic scales are among the most commonly used scales in contemporary popular music. The structure of pentatonic scales is expressed in terms of major scale degrees.

The Major Pentatonic Scale

The major pentatonic scale characterizes the sound of country, bluegrass, and other folk guitar styles, but is also heard in blues, jazz, and heavy metal playing. The scale contains the 1st, 2nd, 3rd, 5th, and 6th degrees of the major scale. The C major pentatonic scale consists of the notes C—D—E—G—A. Fill in the major pentatonic scale chart.

The Minor Pentatonic Scale

The minor pentatonic scale characterizes the sound of blues and rock guitar styles and contains the 1st, flat 3rd, 4th, 5th, and flat 7th degrees of the major scale. The C minor pentatonic scale consists of the notes C–E♭–F–G–B♭. Fill in the minor pentatonic scale chart.

MAJOR PENTATONIC SCALES				
ROOT	SECOND (M2)	THIRD (M3)	FIFTH (P5)	SIXTH (M6)
C	D	E	G	A
G				
D				
A				
E				
B				
F#/Gb				
Db				
Ab				
Eb				
Bb				
F				

Figure 14-1

MINOR PENTATONIC SCALES				
ROOT	FLAT THIRD (b3RD OR m3)	FOURTH (P4)	FIFTH (P5)	FLAT SEVENTH (b7th or m7)
C	Eb	F	G	Bb
G				
D				
A				
E				
B				
F#/Gb				
Db				
Ab				
Eb				
Bb				
F				

Figure 14-2

E Minor Pentatonic in First Position

The E minor pentatonic scale in first position is easy to play and frequently used. Every open string is used, there are only two notes on each string, and the lowest and highest open strings sound the root of the scale.

Neil Young's introduction to "Heart of Gold" contains notes of the E minor pentatonic scale. Use first position chords with open strings, all downstrokes, and hammer-on from the fifth string A to B on the third upbeat of the second measure. Change to Em in the second measure on the second upbeat.

Traditionally, the E minor pentatonic scale is heard over the E, E7, and other chords in the twelve bar blues in E. Tension is created by the contrast between the major third of the E chord and the minor third of the scale.

Link Wray's famous 1958 instrumental, "Rumble," one of the first recordings to use electronically produced reverb and tremolo, is a modified twelve bar blues in E played with open position chords and a descending first position E minor pentatonic scale played in triplets.

The Jimi Hendrix's introduction to "Purple Haze" falls entirely on the notes of an E minor pentatonic scale. In the recording, Hendrix played the notes in higher positions on the neck, up to the ninth fret.

Lonny Mack's recording of "Memphis" is an example of a solo in E using notes

E Minor Pentatonic Scale in First Position

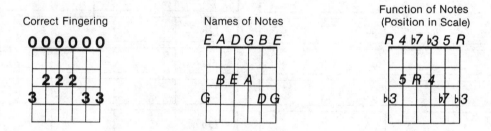

Figure 14-3

Heart of Gold (E Minor Pentatonic Scale with Em Chord)

as recorded by Neil Young   by Neil Young

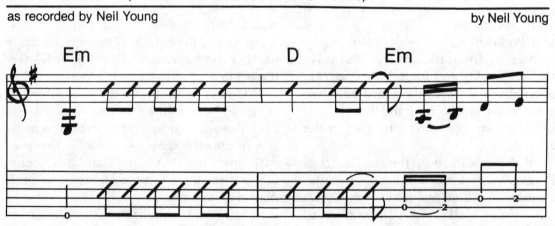

Figure 14-4

found on the open position E minor pentatonic scale. The E minor pentatonic scale can also be heard in the guitar riffs of Led Zeppelin's "How Many More Times" and "Whole Lotta Love."

The Rolling Stones' "Miss You," Steve Miller's "Jet Airliner," and the bass solo of "My Generation" are played on minor pentatonic scales.

G Major Pentatonic

The natural notes G—A—B—D—E form the notes of the G major pentatonic scale. These are the same notes of the E minor pentatonic scale.

The location of the notes and the fingering for the E minor pentatonic scale are the same for the G major pentatonic scale. The notes of the two scales are the same, but each note functions differently. For example, E is the root and the strongest note of the E minor pentatonic scale. At the same time, E is the 6th degree on the G ma-

jor pentatonic, a weaker note which provides tonal color.

Lynyrd Skynyrd uses a G major pentatonic lick in "Sweet Home, Alabama."

The last eight sixteenth notes in the second measure are on the G major pentatonic. Play the introduction as follows:

1. The first two notes are dampened by the edge of the right hand, indicated by the small x under the two D notes.

2. Release pressure on the second sixteenth note G (x) in the second measure immediately after it is struck by the right hand. Do not lift the finger completely off the string.

3. The last note is played at the fifth fret of the third string and bent a whole step to sound as a D (see Chapter 15).

Two Scales, Same Notes

The relationship between the minor pentatonic and major pentatonic scale which

G Major Pentatonic in First Position

Figure 14-5

Sweet Home, Alabama (Introduction: G Major Pentatonic Scale)
as recorded by Lynyrd Skynyrd   Words and Music by Ronnie Van Zant, Ed King & Gary Rossengton

Tablature

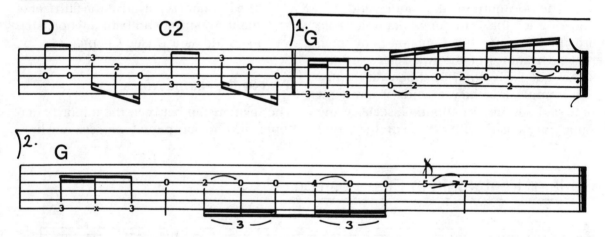

Figure 14-6

share the same notes is as follows:

1. The root of the major pentatonic scale is one and a half steps higher than the root of the minor pentatonic with the same notes.
2. The root of the minor pentatonic is one and a half steps lower than the root of the major pentatonic with the same notes.

For example, A minor pentatonic, A—C—D—E—G, contains the same notes as C major pentatonic. C is one and a half steps above A.

Movable Scale Patterns

A movable scale pattern is a fingering which uses no open strings. Movable patterns allow guitarists to easily transpose riffs and melodies from one key to another. Movable scale patterns, like barre chords, are identified by the string and finger location of the root. Many guitarists use movable scale patterns to create solos.

Movable Pentatonic Scale Patterns

The pattern in Figure 14–7 is played in fifth position. The first finger plays notes on the fifth fret, the third finger plays notes on the seventh fret, and the fourth finger plays notes on the eighth fret.

The notes on the scale form an A minor pentatonic scale and a C major pentatonic scale. As an A minor scale, the root is on the sixth string under the first finger. As a C major scale, the root is on the sixth string under the fourth finger on the eighth fret. Keep in mind the following when practicing the movable pentatonic scale:

1. Finger each note individually. The first finger does not form a barre across all six strings.

2. Play the scale ascending and descending, use all downstrokes, alternate down- and upstrokes, use the thumb, or alternate between index and middle fingers or any other right hand pattern.

3. The notes of the scale create a classic blues or rock and roll sound played against I—IV—V and ♭III—♭VII progressions in A.

4. The notes of the scale create a classic country sound played against I—IV—V progressions in the key of C.

The first measures of Buddy Holly's "That'll Be the Day" (Figure 17–5) and Ernest Tubb's "Walking the Floor Over You" use the same notes found on the fifth position pentatonic scale. The Holly song is in the key of A, while

Movable Pentatonic Scale in Fifth Position

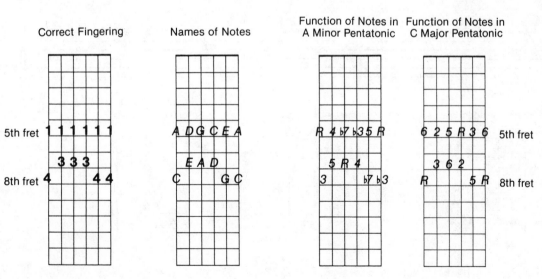

Figure 14-7

True Rock and Roll Improvising Scale

Notes of Minor and Major Pentatonic Scales Combined

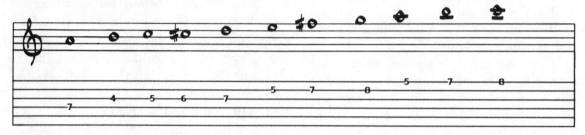

Figure 14-8

Movable Major Scale, Root Sixth String

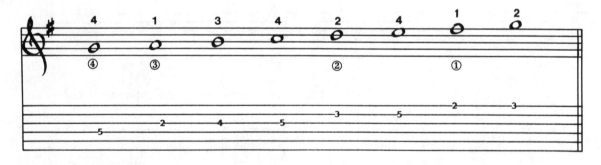

Correct Fingering	Names of Notes	Function of Notes (Position in Scale)

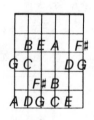
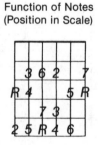

Figure 14-9

Tubb's is in the key of C. Ernest Tubb, incidentally, was one of the first guitarists to introduce electric guitar to the Grand Ole Opry.

The combination of notes found on the major or minor pentatonic scale is the true rock and roll scale. "Johnny B. Goode," "Around and Around," and "That'll Be the Day" (Chapter 17) contain riffs that use notes of the minor and major pentatonic scale with the same root name. Figure 14–8 shows the notes of the A minor pentatonic and the A major pentatonic scales combined.

Movable Major Scale Patterns

The major scales are also used in creating riffs and solos. Every great guitarist has worked out fingerings for the major scales. Most serious guitar students learn several sets of fingerings for the major scales. The following patterns are only two of many.

Figure 14–9 shows a two-octave G major scale played in second position. The root of the scale is played by the second finger on the third fret of the sixth string. The scale is identified as a *root sixth string, movable major scale* pattern. Correct fingering and the names and scale degrees of the notes are shown in grid diagrams.

Figure 14–10 is the D major scale in second position. The root of the scale is played by the fourth finger on the fifth fret of the fifth string. The scale is a *root fifth string, movable major scale* pattern.

The fingering of the scale and the function of each note in the pattern remain the same regardless of where on the neck the pattern is played. Only the names of the notes change when played in different positions.

Movable Major Scale, Root Fifth String

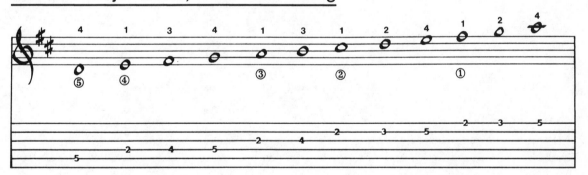

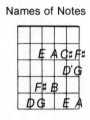 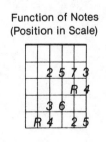

Figure 14-10

Exercises and Projects

1. Memorize the patterns of the movable pentatonic and major scales.

2. Find the notes of all twelve major pentatonic and minor pentatonic scales in first position. This is the source of all pentatonic scale patterns on the guitar.

3. Locate riffs on the G major pentatonic scale in "Ripple" (Figure 5–8).

4. Analyze riffs and solos. Listen and look for major, minor, and pentatonic scales or other scales with which you are familiar.

15

LEAD GUITAR
SPECIAL EFFECTS

Lead guitarists use special effects to add individuality and expression to riffs and solos. These effects include hammer-ons and pull-offs, trills, slides, string bends, and vibrato. Many of these effects are used in the guitar solos transcribed in Chapter 17. Some of the effects are difficult to play accurately and quickly. Work on the exercises and examples below to develop the necessary guitar playing skills. Practice at slow, medium, and fast tempos, but never so fast as to lose control and accuracy.

Hammer-on and Pull-off

Hammers and pulls are used to vary the articulation and accenting of single notes. They are also used to play rapidly, the left hand helping the right hand to sound the notes. *Slurs* are indicated by a curved line over two or more notes. The exercise in Figure 15–1 combines single-note hammer-ons and pull-offs. Every note falls on the fifth position pentatonic scale.

Keep in mind the following when practicing this exercise:

1. The first three notes, G—A—G, are slurred. Strike the first note with the right hand. Hammer-on A with the third finger, then pull-off to G. Keep the first finger on G. The left hand alone sounds A and the second G.
2. All notes are evenly spaced within each group of three and from one beat to another.
3. The second group of three notes are played individually.
4. Leave fingers down as long as possible so that the notes blend into each other.
5. The first finger does not barre across the top four strings.

Grace Notes

A grace note hammer-on is played so quickly it appears to have no duration. The first measure of Figure 15–2 shows evenly spaced hammer-ons. In the second measure the hammer-ons are played as grace notes. Grace notes are indicated by a diagonal slash through the stem of a smaller-than-usual note symbol. Hammer-ons, pull-

Slur Exercise on Movable Pentatonic Scale

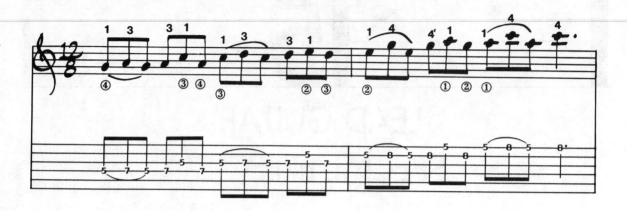

Figure 15-1

Comparison of Grace Note and Evenly Spaced Slurs

Figure 15-2

offs, slides, and string bends can all be played as grace notes. Control the effects so that they can be played either evenly or as grace notes.

Trills

The trill is a very recognizable and flashy technique. In its simplest form, the trill is a combination of hammer-ons and pull-offs, producing a rapid and continuous alternation between two notes. Figure 15–3 shows short trills on two notes, open fourth string D and second fret E.

Keep in mind the following when practicing the trill:

1. Play every note with equal volume and clarity.
2. The trill in example *b* is exactly twice as fast as Example *a*.
3. The trill in Example c is exactly twice as fast as Example *b*.

The number of alternations in a trill depends upon the duration of the note being trilled, the tempo of the song, and the skill of the player.

Slides

A slide is executed by moving the left hand up or down the neck while maintaining pressure on the fretted strings. Slides, like slurs, can be ascending (from low note to high note) or descending (from high note to low), either evenly timed or played as grace notes. The slide is indicated by a straight line connecting two notes. There are grace note slides in "Johnny B. Goode," "Around and Around," "That'll be the Day," and "Get Back" (Chapter 17).

String Bending

String bending is one of the most exciting and challenging guitar techniques. String bending liberates the guitar from the limitations of the frets, which allow only discrete changes in pitch. With string bending, the guitar can produce musical expression as varied and subtle as the human voice.

Bending a string raises its pitch. The further the string is bent, the greater the change in pitch. As in singing, the most important quality of string bending is sustaining an accurate pitch. Listen for accuracy of intonation when practicing string bending techniques.

Whole Step String Bend on the Third String

The following approach develops the strength and tonal accuracy needed to execute clean and effective string bends. The

Trills

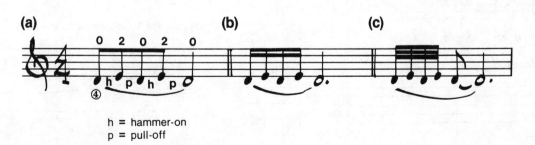

h = hammer-on
p = pull-off

Figure 15-3

techniques applies to bends on all other treble strings. Keep in mind the following when practicing the string bend in Figure 15–4:

1. Establish a target pitch. Place the first finger on the fifth fret of the second string, E. Strike the string.

2. Place the second and third fingers on the sixth and seventh frets of the third string. Strike the third string with the right hand, sounding the D note on the seventh fret.

3. Push the left hand fingers toward the bass side of the neck, bending the third string until it sounds the same pitch as second string E.

4. Do not release the pressure on the string, or the note will be lost. Sustain the bent E note on the third string as long as possible. Do not let the pitch drop.

5. E is also heard at the ninth fret of the third string. Figure 15–4 is an indication to bend the third string seventh fret note so that it sounds like the ninth fret note.

Notation

A string bend is indicated by an arrow between two notes. The note that immediately follows the arrow head indicates the target pitch of a bent note. The note at the beginning of the arrow is the fretted note which is bent to the target pitch. A curved arc over an arrow indicates to not strike the string again at the target note.

Slope

The rate at which a string is bent from one note to another is called the slope. A string bend with a shallow slope changes pitch gradually. A string bend with a sharp slope changes pitch rapidly.

The bend in Figure 15–4 can be played with a shallow or steep slope. To create a shallow slope, begin bending as soon as the D note is struck but bend so slowly that it takes a full beat to raise the pitch of the string all the way to E. Avoid rushing or slowing down the rate of the bend.

To create a sharp slope, let the D sustain for a full beat. Just before the bent E is due to be heard, rapidly bend the third string up a whole step.

Grace Notes and Double Stops

The whole step string bends in Figure 15–5 are all played by the third finger on the seventh fret of the third string. In *b* and *c*, sec-

Whole Step Bend on the Third String

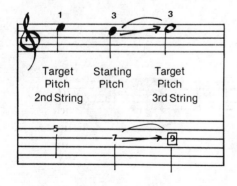

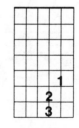

Starting Position

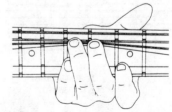

Bending the Third String a Whole Step

Fourth Finger is Near, not on, the Fretboard

Figure 15-4

String Bends

Figure 15-5

ond string, fifth fret E is sounded at the same time as third string, seventh fret D. The first finger plays second string E.

Measure *a* of Figure 15–5 shows a grace note string bend. Bend the third string at the seventh fret to E immediately after striking the string. Do not begin the bend before striking the D note. Grace note string bends have the steepest possible slope.

Play the riff in measure *b* by striking the second string E note at the same time as playing the grace note string bend on the third string. Do not bend the second string note. Hitting two strings at the same time is called a *double stop*.

In measure *c*, third string D is allowed to ring for half a beat before bending up to E.

If a string is to be bent more than once, some way must be found to stop it from ringing while relaxing the string in preparation for the next bend. A bent string can be muted by either the left or right hand. The left hand mutes a bent string by releasing pressure from the string so that it no longer makes contact with the fret board. This pressure release must be done before any falling pitch is heard. A string bend is muted by the right hand by placing the pick on the vibrating string before relaxing the bend.

To play two string bends in a row, first play one, mute with either hand, allow the string to return to its normal position, and then play the second bend. Listen carefully that no unwanted falling pitch is heard.

Blocking, *prebends*, and other string bending techniques are explained in Chapter 17 as they are used in transcribed solos.

Vibrato

Slurs, slides, and bends are techniques used to connect two different notes. Vibrato is a technique used to add interest to a single note. Vibrato is an alternation between a note's pitch and a slight sharpening of that pitch. To add vibrato to a fretted note, maintain strong pressure on the fretboard and slowly push or pull the string just enough to create an audible change in pitch. Return the string to its relaxed position and repeat.

Vibrato varies in depth and speed. The depth of a vibrato is the extent to which the note is sharped. The speed of a vibrato is the rate at which the true pitch and the sharp pitch alternate. Each guitarist uses different depths and speeds of vibrato to create an individual sound.

Vibrato can be added to a sustained string bend. Bend up to a note and hold the target pitch before beginning the vibrato. Add vibrato to an accurate pitch.

Review of Special Effects

Figure 15–6 shows a riff articulated in several different ways with slides, slurs, and string bends. Each variation produces a unique sound. Practice each variation making sure that the rhythm and intonation (pitch) of all notes are correct.

Example *a* uses slides to connect the first three notes and a slur to the fourth note. Example *b* uses hammer-ons and pull-

The Same Notes Played with Different Articulations

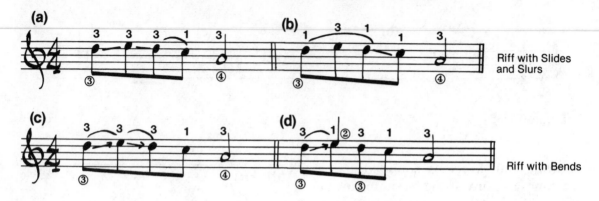

Riff with Slides and Slurs

Riff with Bends

Tablature

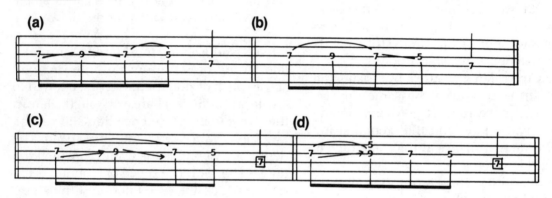

Figure 15-6

offs to connect the first three notes and a slide to the fourth. Example *c* shows an ascending and descending string bend on the third string. Only the first and last notes are struck by the right hand. Be sure to reach the target pitch accurately. In Example *d,* second string E is played at the same time the third string reaches the target pitch. In Example *d* all notes except the second are played by the right hand.

Exercises and Projects

1. Play the movable major scale patterns with slurs, hammer-ons ascending,

and pull-offs descending. Strike each string only once with the right hand. Other notes on the string are played by the left hand. Play all notes evenly.

2. The third string whole step bend from D to E (Figure 15–4) is often played against an A chord. D and E are the 4th and 5th degrees of the A scale. What are the functions, in scale degrees, of the two notes played against C, E, G, D, and F♯ chords?

3. What are the functions of each note in Figure 15–6 in the keys of A, C, D, and E?

4. Play any melody using slurs, slides, and string bends to connect the notes.

16

PATTERNS AND RIFFS
ON THE
HARMONIZED MAJOR SCALES

Guitarists of all styles use harmonized scale patterns to create riffs, solos, and accompaniments. This chapter studies the construction, patterns, and contemporary use of harmonized scales.

Major Scales Harmonized in Thirds

Counting and Playing Thirds on the C Major Scale

In Chapter 10, intervals were formed by the root and each note of the major scale. The size of the interval was measured by counting from the root of the scale to the other note forming the interval. For example, the A note on the C scale forms a 6th with the root. A is the 6th note on the scale, counting from the root.

In this chapter, each note of the scale, in addition to the root, is a starting point for counting intervals. All the notes in Figure 16–1 are on the C major scale.

Figure 16–1a shows how the 3rd degree of the scale is counted from the root. C to E is a M3, or two whole steps. Figure 16–1b shows three notes starting on the 2nd degree of the C scale. D to F is a m3.

Figure 16–1c shows three notes starting on the 3rd degree of the C major scale. E to

Counting Thirds on the C Major Scale

Figure 16-1

G is a m3. The collection of C major scale notes, each harmonized with the scale note a third above it, comprises the C major scale harmonized in thirds, shown in Figure 16–2.

All the notes in Figure 16–2 are on the C major scale. The lower notes are the C major scale from C to C. The upper notes are a 3rd above the lower. Numbers above and below the staff are left hand fingers. Thirds harmonized on the major scales are major third or minor third.

Paul Simon used a riff based on first position C scale notes harmonized in 3rds in "Homeward Bound," as shown in Figure 16–3. The first five pairs of notes are 3rds on

the C major scale in first position. The last double stop is a P4, outlining a G chord.

C Major in Thirds
Played on the Top Two Strings

Find the pattern of thirds on the C major scale as played on the top two strings, as follows:

1. Find all the C scale notes on the second string, from first fret C to thirteenth fret C.
2. Locate all the C scale notes on the first string, from open E up to twelfth fret E.

C Scale Harmonized in Thirds

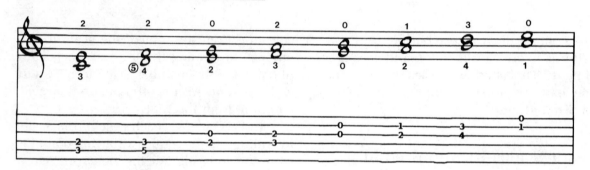

Figure 16-2

Homeward Bound (Introduction: C Scale Harmonized in Thirds)
as recorded by Paul Simon   Words and Music by Paul Simon

Capo Fourth Fret to Play with Recording

Figure 16-3
Copyright ©1966 by Paul Simon. Used by permission.

C Major Scale on the Second String

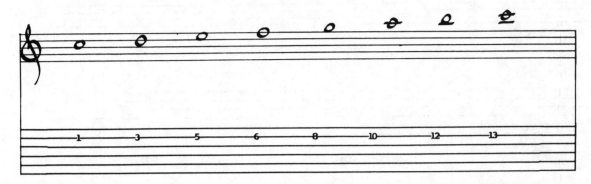

Figure 16-4

C Major Scale Notes on the First String

Figure 16-5

3. Pairs of notes on the top two strings, starting with C on the second string and E on the first, form thirds. Play the strings together, as in Figure 16–6.

Figure 16–6b shows the names of the natural notes on the first and second strings. The grid at *c* shows the note locations grouped in pairs of harmonized 3rds. The grid at *d* shows one possible left hand fingering for playing the C scale harmonized in 3rds on the top strings. The first finger stays on the first string and the second and third fingers form the major and minor third shapes.

Other Major Scales Harmonized in Thirds

The pattern of major thirds and minor thirds on the C major scale is found on all other harmonized major scales. Major scales harmonized in 3rds form a symmetrical pattern. The sequence of 3rds on the first four scale degrees—M3, m3, m3, M3—is the same as the sequence of 3rds on the last four degrees.

Find the pattern of harmonized thirds for any major scales on the top two strings with one of the following methods:

C Scale in Thirds on the Top Two Strings

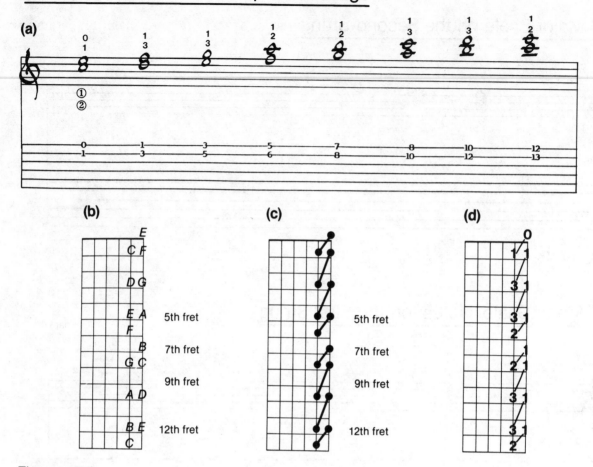

Figure 16-6

Pattern of Thirds on the Major Scales

Thirds on All Major Scales

SCALE DEGREES	C SCALE NOTES	SIZE OF INTERVAL	
		STEPS	THIRD
1 and 3	C and E	2	Major
2 and 4	D and F	1½	minor
3 and 5	E and G	1½	minor
4 and 6	F and A	2	Major
5 and 7	G and B	2	Major
6 and 8	A and C	1½	minor
7 and 9	B and D	1½	minor
8 and 10	C and E	2	Major

Figure 16-7

1. Locate all the scale notes on both strings. Play the strings together, in pairs.
2. Find the root of the scale on the second string. Play the major scale staying on the second string. Preserve the pattern of 3rds on the top two strings, M3—m3—m3—M3—M3—m3—m3— M3, in order to find the first string notes.
3. Start with any scale note on the second string. Identify its position in the scale (scale degree) and play the corresponding major third or minor third with it.

The major third is formed by a note on the second string and the note one fret lower on the first string. The minor third is formed by a note on the second string and the note two frets lower on the first. The shape of major and minor thirds on the first and second strings is seen in the D major and D minor chords.

Figure 16–9 shows the pattern of D major 3rds on the top two strings and the pattern of G major 3rds on the second and third strings.

Major and Minor Third in D and Dm

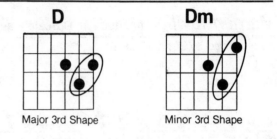

Figure 16-8

D and G in Thirds

(a) D Scale in Thirds

(b) G Scale in Thirds

Figure 16-9

Riffs Using Harmonized Thirds

Figure 16–10 shows the introduction to Jimmy Buffett's "Margarittaville." Every harmonic 3rd falls on the D major scale, the key of the song.

In "Breezin'," the notes of the harmonized 3rds create a variety of coloration and tension with the accompanying chords. For example, C♯ and E in the first measure are the major 7th and 9th of D. In the fourth measure, the same notes function as chord tones, 3rd and 5th, of A7.

In "Brown Eyed Girl," the notes under the G chord are found on the harmonized G major scale and the notes under the C chord are found on the harmonized C major scale. Listen to the introduction to the Rolling Stones' "Wild Horses" for another example of G harmonized in 3rds on the treble strings.

Margarittaville (Introduction: D Scale Harmonized in Thirds)

as recorded by Jimmy Buffett

by Jimmy Buffet

Figure 16-10

Breezin' (Introduction: D Scale Harmonized in Thirds)

as recorded by George Benson

Words and Music by Bobby Womak

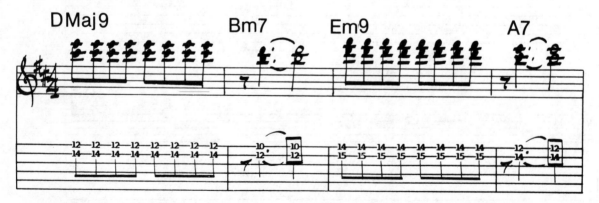

Figure 16-11

Brown Eyed Girl (Introduction: Harmonized Thirds)

as recorded by Van Morrison

Words and Music by Van Morrison

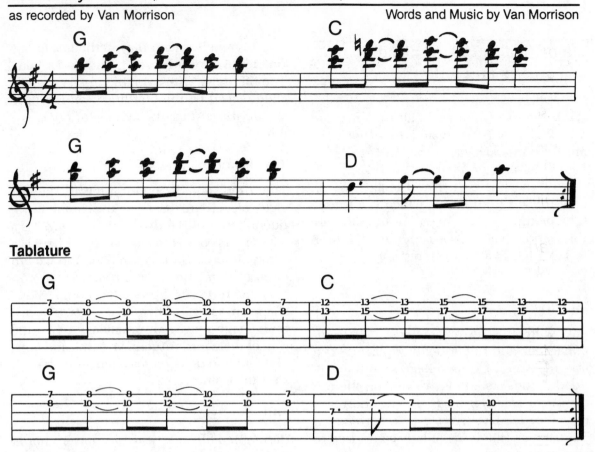

Tablature

Figure 16-12

Figure 16–13 shows a riff based on the G major scale harmonized in 3rds played with double stop hammer-ons and slides. Use the fingering shown in the staff notation. A similar sound is heard in the Eagles' "Lyin' Eyes."

Scotty Moore's solo on Elvis Presley's "That's All Right, Mama" begins with an ascending diatonic bass run and 3rds on the A major scale. Buddy Holly's solo on "It's So Easy" is also composed with 3rds as is the repeated ending of the Pretenders' "Back on the Chain Gang."

G Major Riff in Thirds

Figure 16-13

131

Major Scales Harmonized in Fourths and Fifths

With one exception each, all the 4ths and 5ths found by harmonizing the major scale are the same size, as shown in C major in Figure 16–14.

All the 4ths are two and a half steps except the 4th from F to B, which is a tritone (3T), or three whole steps. All the 5ths are three and a half steps except the 5th from B to F, which is also a tritone.

Fourths

Riffs with 4ths are characteristic of traditional rock and roll lead guitar playing. The first measure of Chuck Berry's "Johnny B. Goode" consists entirely of 4ths on the top two strings (see Figure 17–1). The short guitar solo in Elvis Presley's recording of "Heartbreak Hotel" is similarly comprised of 4ths and played on the top two strings.

George Harrison played the lick in Figure 16–15 in the Beatles' "She Loves You." The riff begins with a double stop grace note slide played by the first finger on the third and fourth strings. Every pair of notes is a 4th.

The Tritone

The tritone is a dissonant interval. The first eight discordant beats of the guitar introduction in Jimi Hendrix's "Purple Haze" is a tritone played on the bass strings. There is a tritone interval between the 3rd and flat 7th of every dominant seventh chord.

Figure 16–16 shows a harmonic tritone shape in several different chords. The tritone shape moves chromatically while the root of the chords ascends by 4ths and 5ths. The function of the notes changes with each shift in position.

Fifths

Harmonic fifths are heard in power chords and rock shuffle patterns. The fifth chords

C Major in Fourths and Fifths

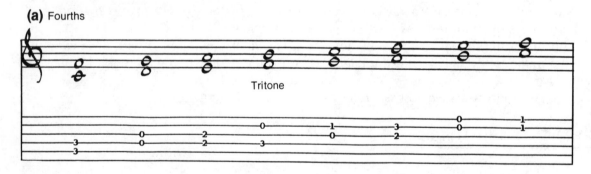

(a) Fourths

Tritone

(b) Fifths

Tritone

Figure 16-14

She Loves You (Riff in Fourths)

as recorded by The Beatles   (written by John Lennon & Paul McCartney)

Figure 16-15

Harmonic Tritones

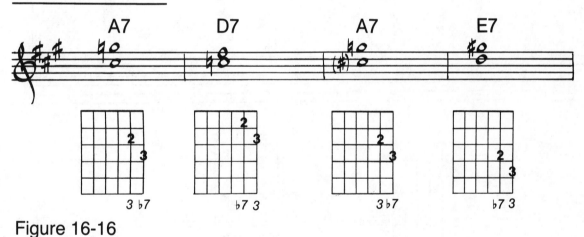

Figure 16-16

shown at the bottom of Chord Chart 2 (Figure 1–5) are constructed with only the root and 5th of the major scale. There is no major third, minor third, or any other scale degree.

Major Scales Harmonized in Sixths

The major scales harmonized in 6ths produce intervals of varying size. The melodic quality of 6ths makes them a popular device in many styles of contemporary music. Figure 16–17 shows one octave of C major scale notes harmonized in sixths starting on the bass strings in first position.

Paul Simon made extensive use of scales in 6ths in "Bookends," "Kathy's Song," and "I am a Rock." Paul McCartney's "Hot as Sun" uses diatonic and chromatic 6ths. Chuck Berry's recording of "Memphis" and Steve Cropper's playing on "Dock of the Bay" also illustrate the sound of harmonized 6ths.

C Major in Sixths

Figure 16-17

C Major in Sixths on the Treble Strings

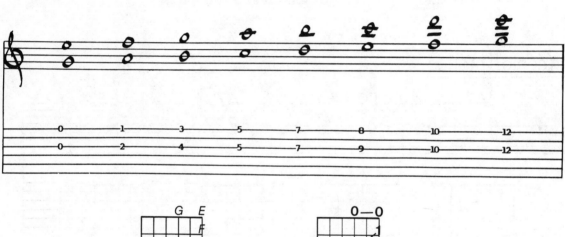

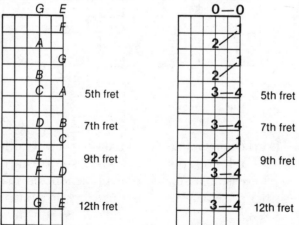

Figure 16-18

Sixths on the Treble Strings

Find the pattern of C major scale notes harmonized in 6ths and played on the treble strings as follows:

1. Locate C major scale notes on the first and third strings.
2. Play the scale notes on the first and third strings together in pairs, starting with the open first and third strings, as in Figure 16–18. The G and E strings are tuned a sixth apart.

Similarly, locate E major notes on the first and third strings to play the E major harmonized in 6ths pattern, as in Figure 16–19.

Guitar Riffs
Using Harmonized Sixths

The guitar introduction to Paul Simon's "Was a Sunny Day" contains several examples of harmonized 6ths on the C major scale.

Keep in mind the following when playing the guitar part in Figure 16–20:

1. Hold down and sustain the lower note of each pair of sixths. Every note in the first two measures is played on the pattern of C major scale notes harmonized in 6ths.
2. The second finger slides on the third string for the first four measures.

E Major In Sixths

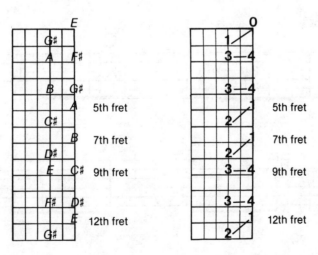

Figure 16-19

3. The notes in the third and fourth measures form a G chord, played with a D major shape in seventh position.

All the notes in Steve Cropper's "Soul Man" introduction in Figure 16–21 are played by the second finger on the third string and the third finger on the first string. Every note is on the E major scale except the D natural at the beginning of the third measure. D is the flat 7th of the E scale. Add a slow vibrato to the long notes.

The fingerpicking blues riff in Figure 16–22 is played with the second, third, and fourth fingers. The second finger alternates between bass strings, the third finger stays on the third string, and the fourth finger stays on the first string. The right hand thumb plays the bass notes and the index and middle fingers pluck the treble strings.

Figure 16–23 shows a shuffle pattern variation on the bass strings.

Was A Sunny Day (Introduction: Riff in Harmonized Sixths)

as recorded by Paul Simon

Words and Music by Paul Simon

Tablature

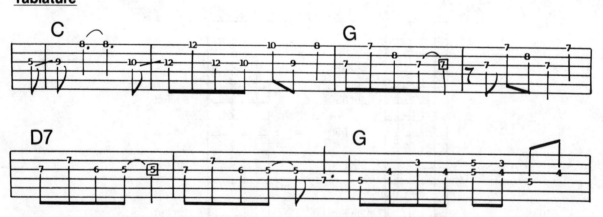

Figure 16-20

Soul Man (Introduction: Riff in Harmonized Sixths)

as recorded by Steve Cropper with The Blues Brothers

by David Porter & Isaac Hayes

Tablature

Figure 16-21

An E Blues Riff Using Sixths

Figure 16-22

Shuffle Pattern Using Sixths

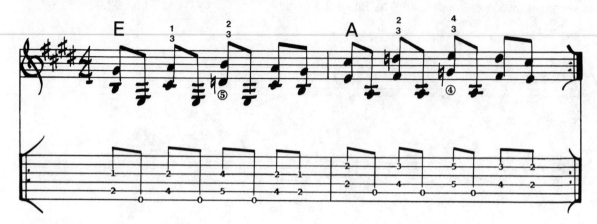

Figure 16-23

Compound Intervals

Intervals larger than an octave are called compound intervals. The 8th degree of a scale, or octave, has the same letter name as the root. Likewise, the 9th degree has the same letter name as the 2nd degree.

Figure 16–24a shows thirteen notes of the C major scale. Figure 16–24b shows compound harmonic intervals on the C scale.

Tenths

The compound interval of an octave plus a third is called a tenth. Tenths are often used to embellish a fingerpicking accompaniment. For example, the Beatles' "Blackbird" is a study in harmonic 10ths. A transcription

Counting Compound Intervals

(a)

(b)

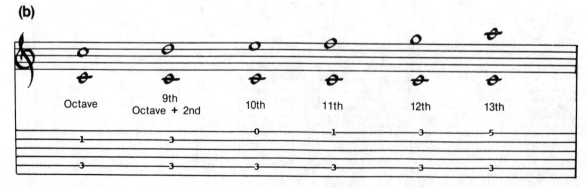

Figure 16-24

G Scale in Tenths

Figure 16-25

can be found in the August 1984 issue of *Guitar for the Practicing Musician*. Figure 16–25 shows a pattern of harmonized 10ths in the key of G.

Jim Croce's "Time in a Bottle" contains an arpeggio picking pattern in ¾ time, a chromatically descending bass line under a minor chord, and a bass run harmonized in 10ths.

Exercises and Projects

1. Locate and memorize the pattern of 3rds and 6ths on the treble strings for any key and for all twelve major scales.

2. The pattern of major and minor 3rds on the harmonized major scale is M3—m3—m3—M3—M3—m3—m3—M3. What is the pattern of major and minor 6ths on the harmonized major scales?

3. Listen and look for patterns of harmonized major scales in your own licks, solos, accompaniments, and arrangements.

17

TRANSCRIBED GUITAR SOLOS

"Johnny B. Goode"

Figure 17–1 is a transcription of the introduction to "Johnny B. Goode," as originally recorded by Chuck Berry. This is one of the most famous songs of all time. In 1977 the Voyager 2 space rocket was launched containing a recording of Bach, Beethoven, Stravinsky, a sampling of music from all over the world, and Chuck Berry's "Johnny B. Goode."

Keep in mind the following when practicing this guitar part:

1. Following the pickup measure, the eighth notes are played in groups of three. The grouping is accentuated by the grace note double stop slide. Each eighth note lasts half a beat.

2. The single-note runs fall on a combination of the B♭ minor pentatonic and B♭ major pentatonic scales.

3. Starting in the fifth measure, a grace note slide to F on the tenth fret of the third string alternates with F played on the sixth fret of the second string.

4. The syncopated F note riff is played over the IV chord (E♭) in measures 5 and 6, and over the I chord (B♭)in measures 7 and 8.

5. Use all downstrokes.

"Around and Around"

Figures 17–3 and 17–4 are transcriptions of the guitar parts as played by the Rolling Stones and recorded on their *12×5* album. The song is a twelve bar blues progression in A.

Use the first finger to hold down third string B and the second finger to hold down second string E in the introduction *a*. The first and second fingers stay down on their strings. Do not let the second finger touch the first string. Alternate down- and up-strokes, down on the third string, up on the first, down on the second string, up on the first. Keep the third finger on sixth fret C♯ as long as possible.

The two guitars at *b* establish a pattern that is repeated throughout the progression. Keep in mind the following:

140

Johnny B. Goode (Introduction)

as recorded by Chuck Berry

Words and Music by Chuck Berry

Figure 17-1

Johnny B. Goode (Tab)

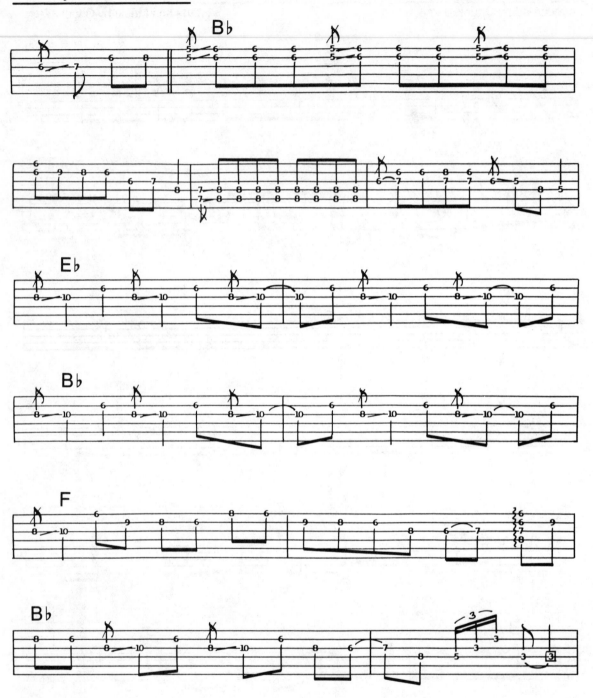

Figure 17-2

Around and Around (Rhythm and Lead Guitar Parts)

as recorded by The Rolling Stones

Words and Music by Chuck Berry

(a)

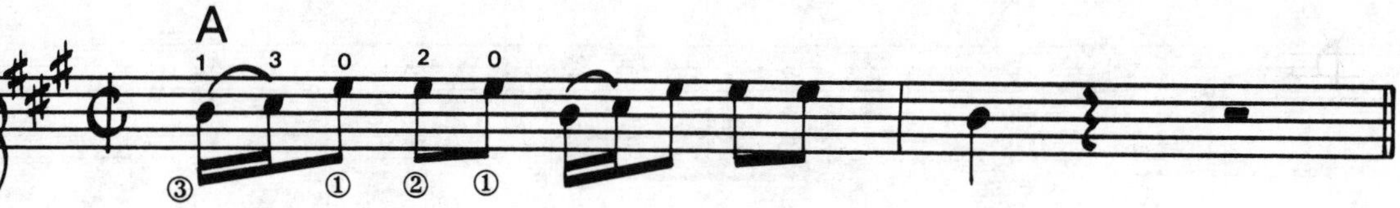

(b)

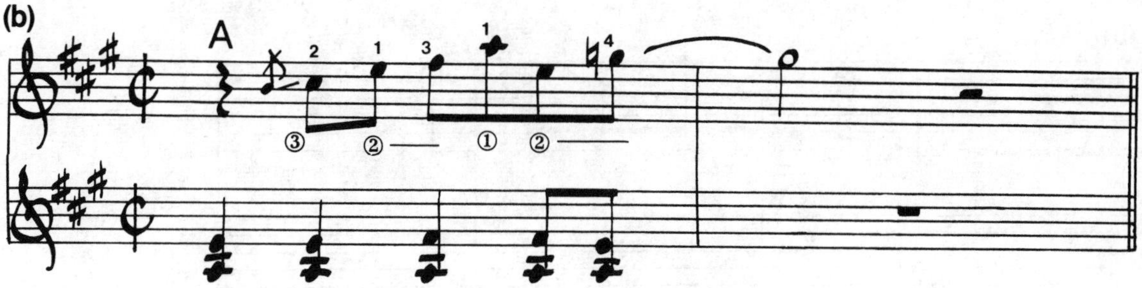

(c)

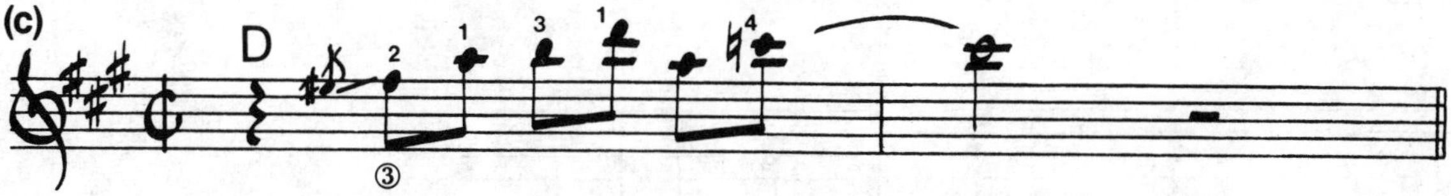

(d)

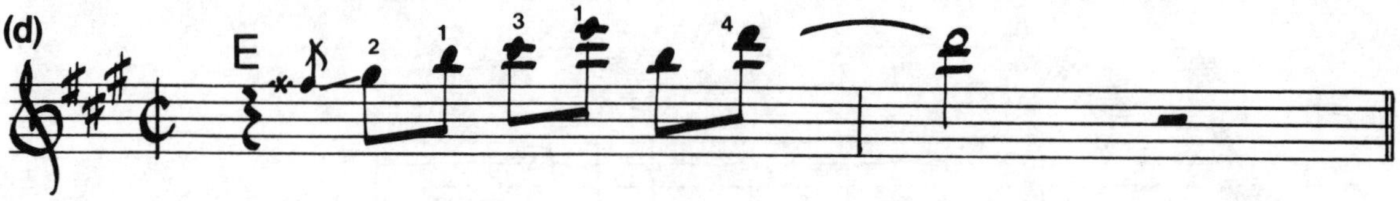

(e)

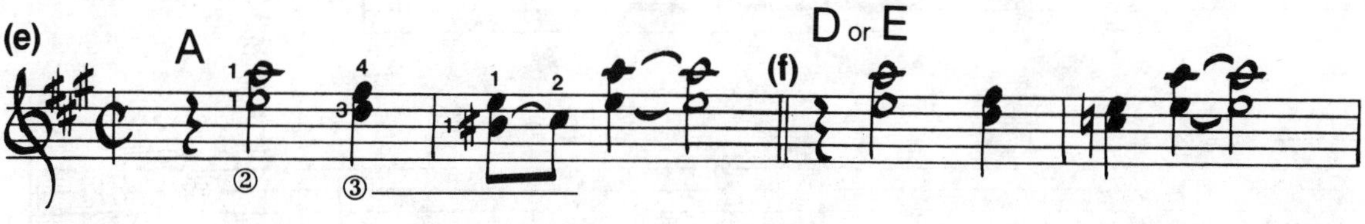

(g)

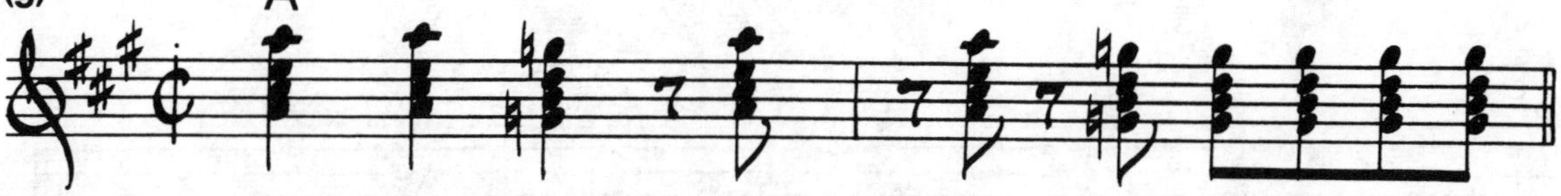

(h)

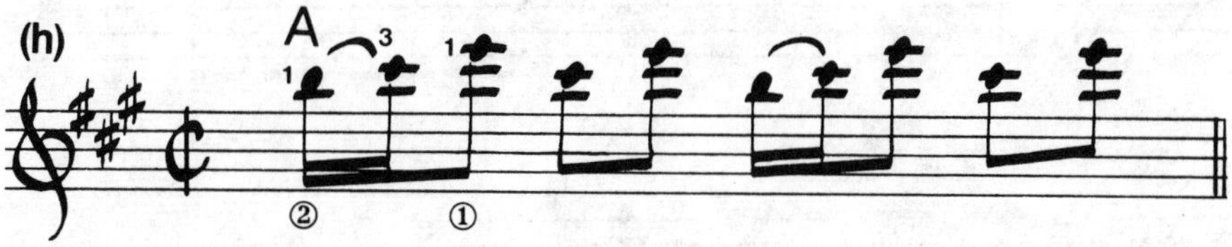

Figure 17-3

Around and Around (Tab)

Figure 17-4

1. The rhythm guitar (lower line) plays a variation on the traditional rock shuffle pattern. Dampen the strings after striking the last upbeat of the measure. All the rhythm licks are played on the fifth and fourth strings.
2. The lead guitar part is played in fifth position.
3. The grace note slide on the third string is played by the left hand second finger.
4. Hold down a small barre on the top two strings.
5. Alternate down and upstrokes. The last note is an upstroke.

The riff in A is transposed to D and E by playing higher on the neck. The measures at *c* and *d* show the lead guitar part transposed to the IV chord D, and V chord (E). The fingering, timing, and functions of the notes are the same. Transpose the rhythm guitar part to D and E using the root fifth string movable shuffle pattern (see Figure 12–6).

The measures at *e* show another lead guitar part. The lick is played throughout the twelve bar progression with only slight modification, as shown by the measures at *f*.

1. Use a first finger small barre on the top three strings.
2. The second pair of notes, F♯ and D, are fingered by the third and fourth fingers of the left hand.
3. The hammer-on from C to C♯ in the second measure is played evenly. The two notes have the same half-beat duration.
4. Play all the notes with upstrokes.

The single note run in *b* is transposed for each chord. The notes change while the function (sound) of the notes stays the same. The double stop lick in *f* is repeated over the chord changes. The notes stay the same while the function (sound) of the notes changes with each chord.

Here is how the notes of the lick in Figure 17–3e function in A:

1. A and E are the root and 5th of A.
2. F♯ and D are the 6th and 4th of A.
3. E and C are the 5th and flat 3rd. The hammer-on to C♯ is from the minor third to the major third of the chord.

The lick contains the root, 3rd and 5th of the A major chord, and also the 4th and 6th of the A major scale.

Here is how the notes in Figure 17–3f function against the D chord:

1. A and E are the 5th and 9th.
2. F♯ and D are the 3rd and root.
3. E and C are the 9th and flat 7th.

The lick contains the root, 3rd, 5th, flat 7th, and 9th of a D9 chord.

Here is how the same notes function against the E chord:

1. A and E are the 4th and root.
2. F♯ and D are the 9th and flat 7th.
3. E and C are the root and sharp 5th.

There are fewer strong chord tones: the notes of the lick spell an E11♯5 chord.

The chord riff in Figure 14–3g is transposed to D and E by playing in higher positions.

The hammer-on riff in *h* is used late in the song and echoes the introduction an octave higher. The riff is played in twelfth position. Place a small barre across the top two strings at the twelfth fret and hammer-on to the fourteenth fret with the third finger. Use alternate up- and downstrokes.

"That'll Be the Day"

This was Buddy Holly's first hit record. Even though he was not as popular as Elvis, Buddy Holly was the more proficient, innovative, and imitated first generation rock and roll guitarist.

That'll Be the Day (Guitar Solo)

as recorded by Buddy Holly

by Norman Petty, Buddy Holly & Joe Allison

Figure 17-5

That'll Be the Day (Tab)

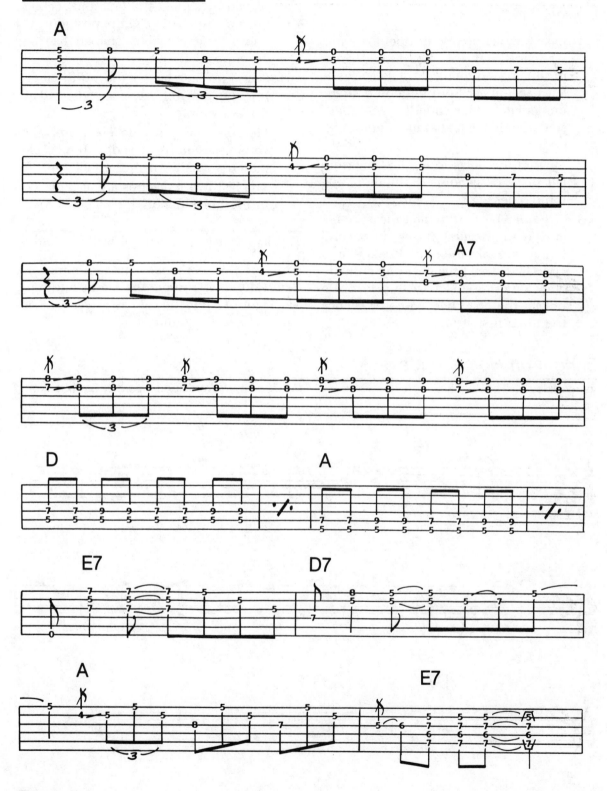

Figure 17-6

Keep in mind the following when playing the solo:

1. Rake the pick across the opening A major chord on the top four strings, producing a rippling effect. Release the left hand finger from the chord shape immediately after sounding the chord so that only the first string A note rings out.

2. Most of the notes in the first measure fall on a descending A minor pentatonic blues scale.

3. The third beat of the first measure begins with the first finger on second string D♯. Strike the fretted second and open first strings together and immediately slide the first finger up to E. Do not let the first finger mute or silence the open first string.

4. The last beat of the third measure is played by sliding the first and second fingers into an eighth position A7 chord. The chord is shaped like an open position D7.

5. Slide into each beat of the fourth measure from one fret below, as indicated by the grace notes.

6. Measures five through eight are rock shuffle variations played with movable patterns as shown in the tablature.

7. The last two measures are also played in the introduction.

"Bring It on Home to Me"

This song was originally made popular by Sam Cooke, who wrote the words and music. Figure 17–4 is the solo as played by Eric Burdon and the Animals.

Bring It on Home to Me (Solo)

as recorded by The Animals   Words and Music by Sam Cooke

Figure 17-7

Bring it on Home to Me (Tab)

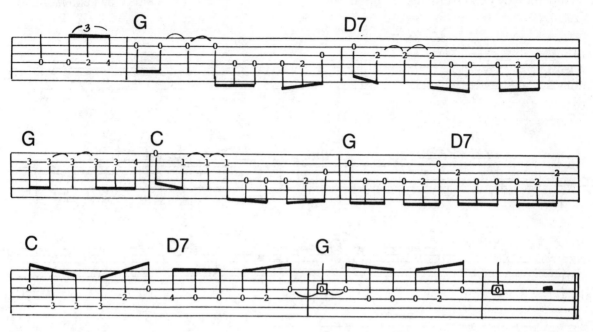

Figure 17-8

This solo illustrates the use of a major scale in constructing an improvisation. The notes of the solo hint at the melody or sketch the chord progression by emphasizing strong chord notes. Except for D♯ in the third measure, every note is on the G major scale. All groups of three-beamed eighth notes are triplets.

"Steel Guitar Rag"

This song was recorded in 1936 by Bob Wills and his Texas Playboys. Bob Wills' band played a mixture of country, blues, and jazz, and in the 1930s and early 1940s was the most influential band in the southwest.

The solo was played by steel guitarist Leon McAuliffe. Steel guitar is played with a metal slide to change the pitch of the strings, creating continual transitions from one note to another. The regular six string guitar is designed to change notes by discrete intervals.

Guitar technique has often evolved as guitar players attempted to imitate the sounds and textures of other instruments. "Steel Guitar Rag" popularized the sound of steel guitar and was a source of inspiration for the technique of half step and whole step string bends.

The measure before the double bar is a half step bend of two notes forming a m6. The bend is into E chord notes. Slide into the E chord notes if it is too difficult to accurately bend notes on two strings at the same time.

Except for the half step bend to G natural, all the notes fall on the E major pentatonic scale. When playing the string bends, keep the first finger on the fifth fret of the second string and bend the note as indicated at the seventh fret with the third finger. The first three string bends are half step bends from F♯ to G. The bend in measure 7 is a whole step to G♯. Sustain G♯ while playing the first string B at the seventh fret.

The E major chord arpeggio in measures 5 and 9 falls on the root fifth string movable major scale pattern.

Steel Guitar Rag (Steel Guitar Solo)

as recorded by Leon McAuliffe with Bob Wills

Music by Leon McAuliffe

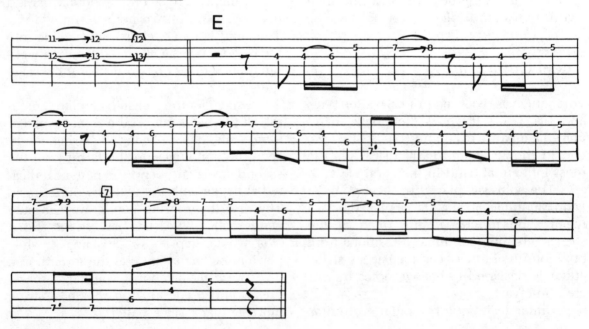

Figure 17-9
©1944 by Bourne Co. Copyright renewed. Used by permission.

Steel Guitar Rag (Tab)

Figure 17-10

"Get Back"

The solo begins with a grace note slide from the ninth to eleventh fret on the third string. Use the second finger. This puts the left hand in tenth position, ready to play the whole step bend on the second string at the end of the measure. Prepare the fourth finger on the twelfth fret of the first string. Sustain the string bend to C♯ through the first string E note in preparation for the descending bend in the second measure.

The third measure begins with a grace note slide on the fifth string from the seventh to ninth frets. Use the third finger. The D note on the third string is played with the first finger, as is the C natural. Shift to fifth position to play the C note. Bend the C a half step to C♯ at the beginning of the fourth measure.

The solo uses mostly major pentatonic scale notes. The riff under the A chord falls on the A major pentatonic scale, and the riff under the D chord falls on the D major pentatonic scale, except for the C note. C is the flat 7th of D and also the flat 3rd of A. The half step bend between measures three and four is from the m3 to M3 of A.

Get Back (Guitar Solo)

as recorded by The Beatles

Words and Music by John Lennon & Paul McCartney

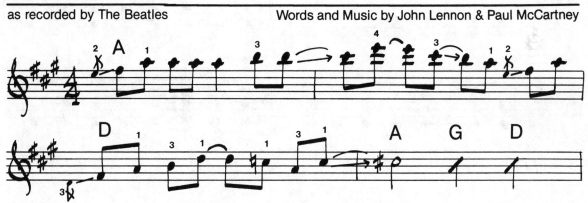

Figure 17-11

Get Back (Tab)

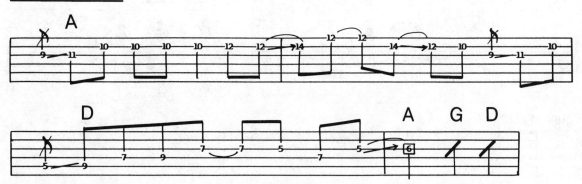

Figure 17-12

"Back in the USSR"

Figures 17–13 and 17–14 show some of the rhythm and lead guitar riffs used in the Beatles' recording.

The measures at *a* are shuffle patterns played on the I, ♭III, and IV chords in A. Measures at *b* are fingered the same but played in different positions; the notes are found on the rock and roll scale. Measure *c* is the chromatically ascending chords used at the end of the verses.

The string bends in measure *d* are from George Harrison's solo. Except for the last three As, all notes are played on the second string. The solo calls for seven repetitions of a whole step string bend on the second string. Block the string immediately before each string bend repetition. Place the pick on the string to stop it from vibrating so that no falling pitch is heard.

Back in The U.S.S.R. (Guitar Parts)

as recorded by The Beatles   Words and Music by John Lennon & Paul McCartney

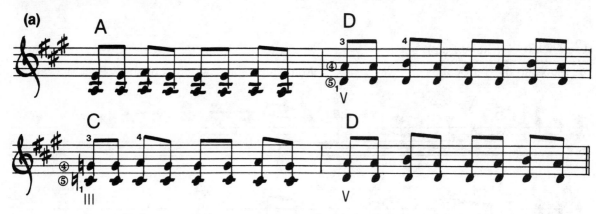

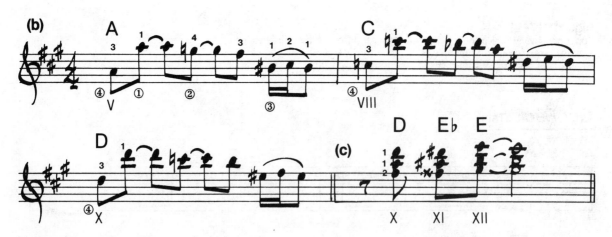

Figure 17-13

The D—E—D eighth and sixteenth note lick in the third measure is an ascending whole-step string bend followed by a descending whole step string bend. All three notes are played at the fifteenth fret by the third finger. Play the notes without string bends to hear the correct pitch and bends to hear the correct pitch and timing.

Section *e* is a continuation of the solo.

Prebends are used starting in the second measure. Finger thirteenth fret C, the string with the pick, and prebend the string to D, without sounding any notes. The string can now be played as a D at the thirteenth fret and bent down to C, as indicated in the transcription. Play the notes in the second and third measures without bends to hear the correct pitch and timing.

Back in the U.S.S.R. (Continued)

Figure 17-14

Back in The U.S.S.R. (Tab)

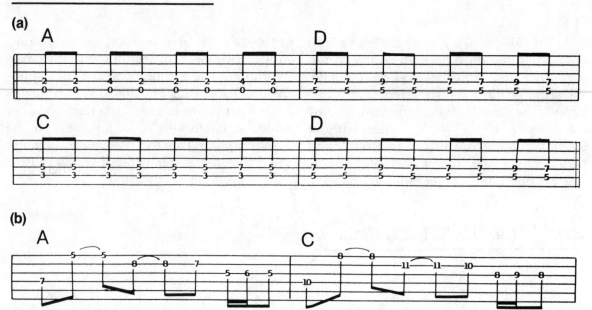

Figure 17-15

Back in the U.S.S.R. (Tab, Continued)

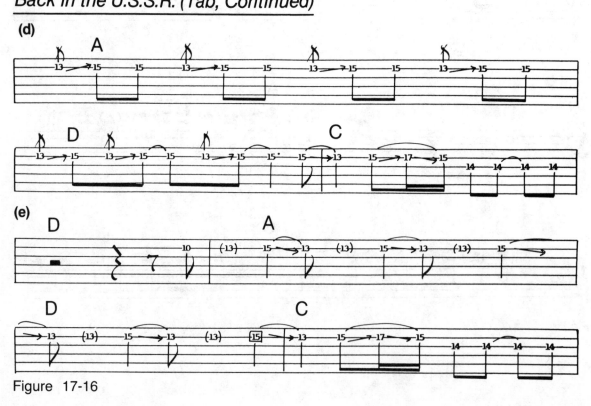

Figure 17-16

Exercises and Projects

1. Memorize the transcribed solos in this chapter.

2. Analyze each solo. What are the names of the notes played in each lick? What are the harmonic functions (scale degrees) of each note? Which scale degrees predominate in the riffs and solos, chord tones, passing tones or altered tones?

3. Play the solos in different positions on the guitar. For example, find the notes of "Bring it On Home to Me" on a movable G major scale pattern and vary the articulation and accents with slurs and slides. Transpose an octave higher and play with string bends.

4. Play the solos along with the original recordings.

5. Transpose the solos to different keys.

18

CHORD VOCABULARY

This chapter focuses on improving chord vocabulary using a system of chord construction based on the major scales. The spelling of major, minor, and seventh chords was introduced in Chapter 10. With this system, guitar players can find the voicing and fingering of each new chord as it is needed.

Building and Improving Chord Vocabulary

Alterations and Extensions

Complex chords are best understood as alterations and extensions of simple chord structures. A chord is altered by changing one of its notes. For example, the augmented chord is formed by raising the 5th degree of the major triad a half step: The augmented chord is an alteration of the major chord. A chord is extended by adding a note. For example, the major sixth is formed by adding the sixth degree of the major scale to the major triad: The major sixth is an extension of the major chord.

Chord alterations and extensions add color to simple chords. They are used to make progressions more interesting, to create voicings that blend into one another, and to harmonize melodies in which important melody notes do not fall on chord notes or even on scale degrees.

Families of Chord Types

The three common chord types—major, minor, and seventh—also form the basis of three families of chord sounds. With a few exceptions, all other chord types can be understood as extensions and alterations of the major, minor, and dominant seventh chords.

The following chord types are extensions of the C major triad: Major sixth (C6), major seventh (CMaj7), major six/nine (C6/9), major added ninth (Cadd9), major ninth (CMaj9).

These chord types are extensions of the C minor triad: minor sixth (Cm6), minor seventh (Cm7), minor ninth (Cm9).

Extensions and alterations of the C dominant seventh chord include: ninth (C9), eleventh (C11), thirteenth (C13), seventh flat five (C7♭5), seventh sharp five (C7♯5), seventh sharp nine (C7♯9).

Complex chords can be simplified. For

example, CMaj9 can be simplified to C major, Cm11 can be simplified to C minor, and C13 can be simplified to C7.

Chord charts in this chapter present the spelling, voicing, shape, and fingering of common chord extensions and alterations. The charts are organized by chord type. Open string, barre, and other movable voicings are given. The harmonic function of the notes in the chords is shown below the grid diagrams. The root is identified by the letter R. Position movable chords so that the note on the root string is the same as the name of the chord.

Simple Extensions and Alterations of Triads

The maj6, maj7, m7, sus4, and sus2 chords are formed by adding one note to a major or minor triad, or by changing only one note of the chord.

These chord types are easy to voice using common open position and barre major and minor chords. Add or change the note of the chord shape according to the chord formula for each type. This system of chord construction requires knowledge of the names of notes on the fretboard, the notes of the major scales, and the function of each note in common chord shapes.

Major Sixth

The major sixth is used primarily as a variation of the major triad.

Major Seventh

The major seventh is a variation on the major triad. The major seventh is different from

Chord Chart: Major Sixths

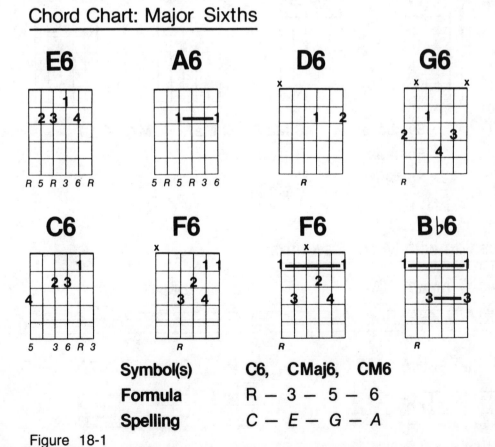

Symbol(s)	C6, CMaj6, CM6
Formula	R — 3 — 5 — 6
Spelling	C — E — G — A

Figure 18-1

the dominant or regular seventh. The major seventh chord is formed by adding the seventh degree of the major scale to the major triad. The dominant seventh chord is formed by adding the flatted 7th degree to the major triad. Listen to "Misty" (Errol Garner), "Girl from Ipanema" (A.C. Jobim), and "Fifty Ways to Leave Your Lover" (Paul Simon) for examples of the Maj7 sound.

A major chord is changed to Maj7 by lowering a root note a half step to the seventh degree. A half step is one fret. For example, open position C major becomes CMaj7 by lifting the first finger off the second string. The Maj7 is sometimes used as a passing chord between major and dominant seventh chords, as in Figure 18–3. Listen to George Harrison's "Something" for an example of the major—Maj7—dominant seventh progression.

Chord Chart: Major Sevenths

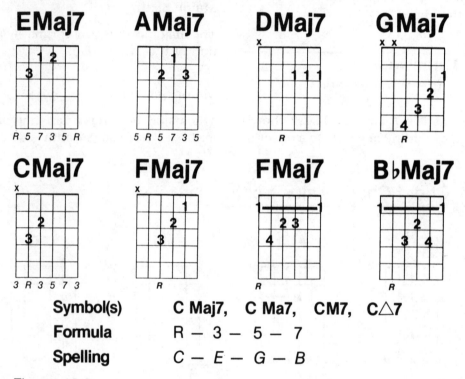

Symbol(s)	C Maj7, C Ma7, CM7, C△7
Formula	R − 3 − 5 − 7
Spelling	C − E − G − B

Figure 18-2

Progression with Major Sevenths

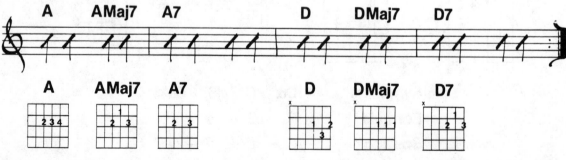

Figure 18-3

Minor Seventh

The minor seventh chord is formed by adding a flatted seventh degree to the minor triad. The minor triad and minor seventh are similar in sound.

Each minor seventh chord has the same notes as a major sixth chord whose root is a minor 3rd higher. For example, Am7 has the same notes, A—C—E—G, as C6, which is spelled C—E—G—A. Am7 and C6 are different names for the same collection of notes. The two chords are chord synonyms and can sometimes substitute for each other in progressions.

The minor seventh can also substitute for a dominant seventh chord whose root is a perfect fourth higher. For example, four beats of G7 can be played as two beats of Dm7 and two beats of G7. The substitution works because the notes of the minor seventh are either part of, or very close to, the notes of the dominant seventh.

In Figure 18–5, Am7 and D7 substitute for a measure of D7, and Dm7 and G7 substitute for a measure of G7. The chord grids at *c* are voicings on the bass strings. The grids at *d* are voicings played on the treble strings.

Sus4

The *sus* of sus4 is short for *suspended*. In sus4 chords, the 4th degree of the scale replaces the 3rd in the construction of the triad. Since there is no 3rd degree in the sus4 chord it is neither major nor minor.

The sus4 is used as a variation on a major chord, as in the introduction to "Brown Sugar" shown in Figure 18–7.

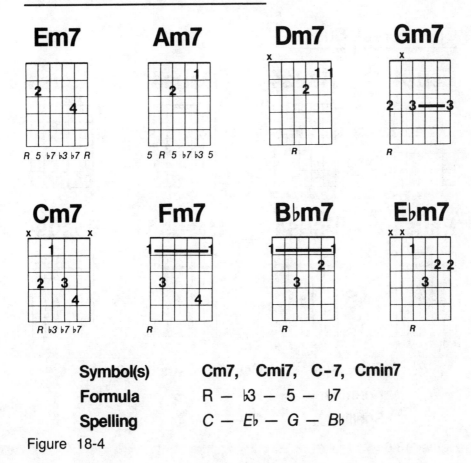

Chord Chart: Minor Sevenths

Symbol(s)	Cm7, Cmi7, C–7, Cmin7
Formula	R — ♭3 — 5 — ♭7
Spelling	C — E♭ — G — B♭

Figure 18-4

Chord Substitutions with **IIm7 V7**

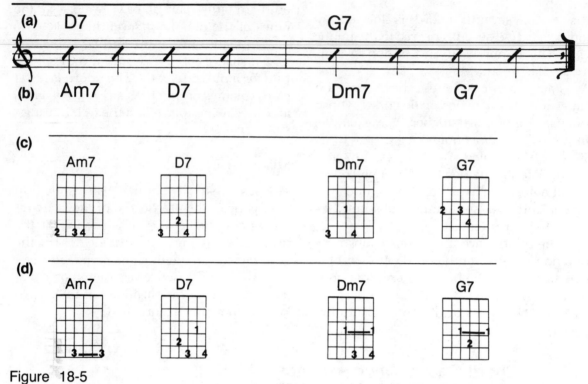

Figure 18-5

Chord Chart: Sus4

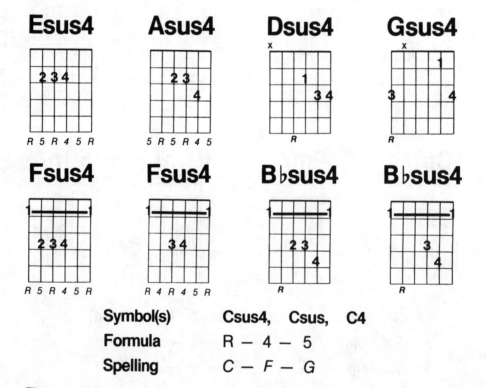

Symbol(s)	Csus4, Csus, C4
Formula	R – 4 – 5
Spelling	C – F – G

Figure 18-6

Brown Sugar (Introduction: Sus4 Chords)

as recorded by The Rolling Stones — Words and Music by Mick Jagger and Keith Richards

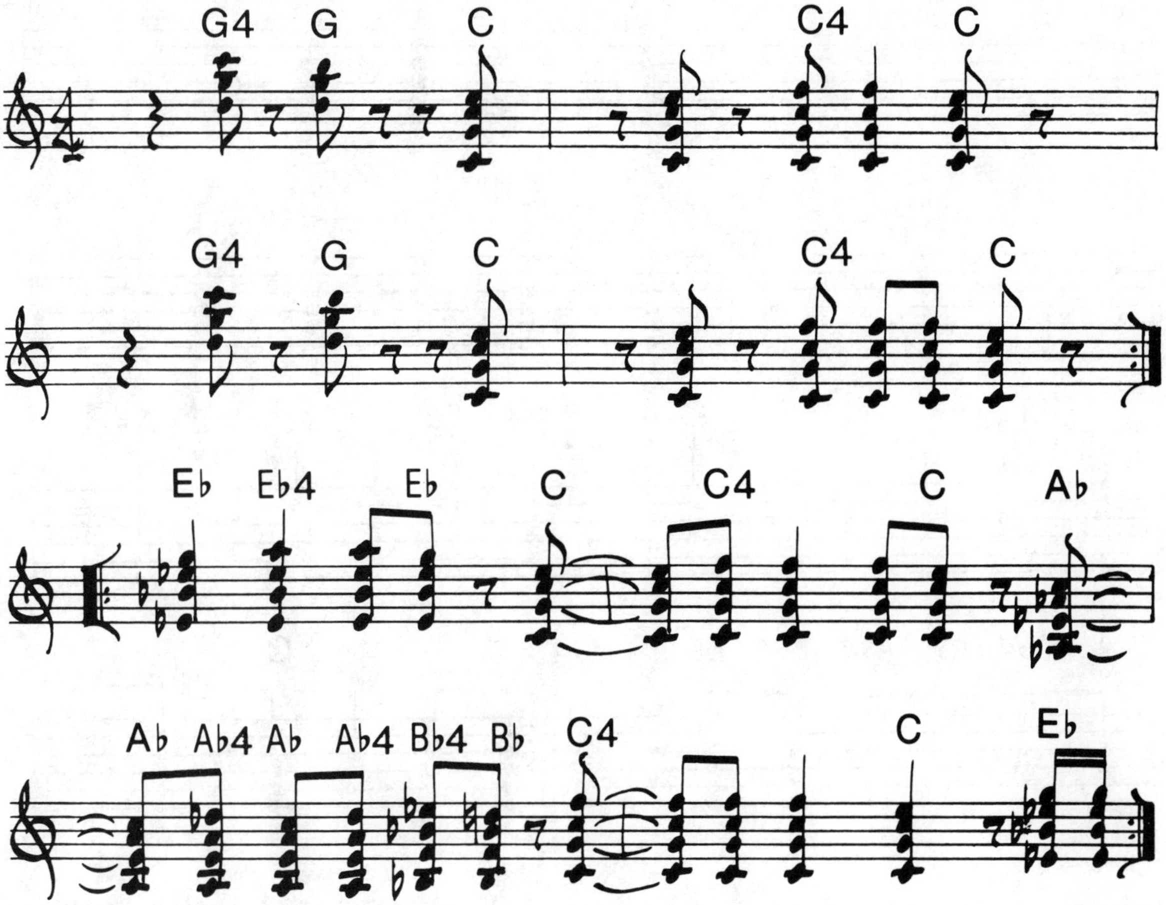

Figure 18-7

Brown Sugar (Tab)

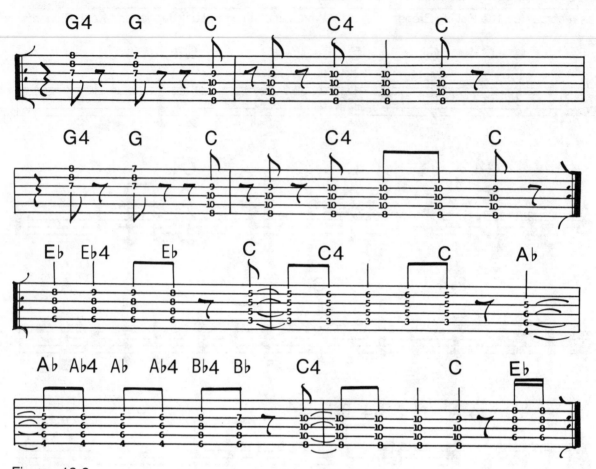

Figure 18-8

Keep in mind the following while working on this guitar part:

1. The first chord is a D major shape played at the seventh fret with the fourth finger added to the first string. Play G4 and G with upstrokes.

2. The C chords in the first half are root sixth string barre chord shapes in eighth position.

3. The E♭ and C chords in the third line are root fifth string barre chord shapes in sixth and third position.

4. All other chords are root sixth string shapes.

Other songs with sus4 chords include "Pinball Wizard" and "Needle and the Damage Done." "Walking in Your Footsteps," by the Police, is based on an alternation between a major chord and its sus4.

Leonard Cohen used suspended fourth chords in "Suzanne." The picking pattern for each chord is shown in Figure 18–9. The thumb and index fingers alternate on three bass strings while the middle finger plays sustained chord tones. Follow the chord progression on the recording.

Suzanne (Finger Picking Pattern)

as recorded by Leonard Cohen

Words and Music by Leonard Cohen

Figure 18-9

Suzanne (Tab)

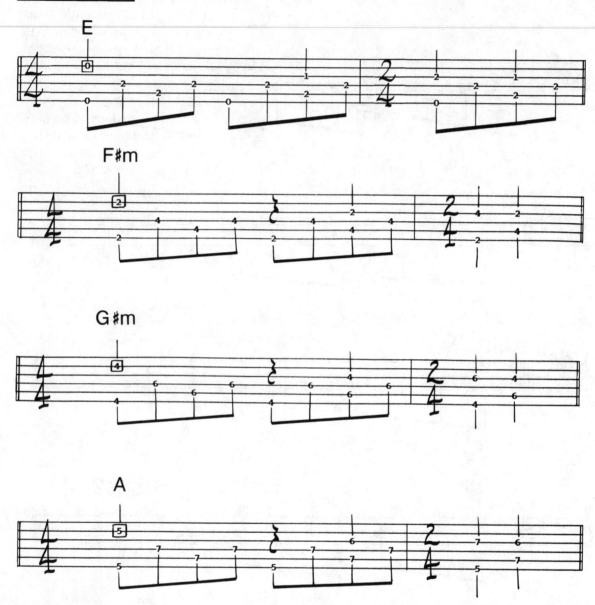

Figure 18-10

Sus2 and Add9

In the sus2 chord, the 2nd degree of the scale replaces the 3rd degree of the triad. The sus2, like the sus4, is neither major nor minor. The add9 chord is a major triad with the 9th degree added. The add9 chord is sometimes called an add2, since the 9th is the same note as the 2nd.

The notes of sus2 chords spell at least one other chord. For example, the notes of Asus2, A—B—E, also spell Esus4 and are found in Bm11. "You've Got to Hide Your Love Away" and "Dust in the Wind" use sus4, sus2, and add9 chords.

Other Chord Types

The diminished triad is spelled with the root, flat 3rd and flat 5th of the major scale. C diminished triad is written Cdim. The augmented triad is spelled with the root, 3rd, and sharp 5th. The sharp 5th degree is also called the augmented 5th. C augmented triad is written C aug or C+.

The minor sixth chord is formed by adding the 6th degree of the major scale to a minor triad. The use of the minor sixth chord is explored at the end of this chapter in the section on half-diminished seventh chords.

Chord Chart: Sus2 and Add9

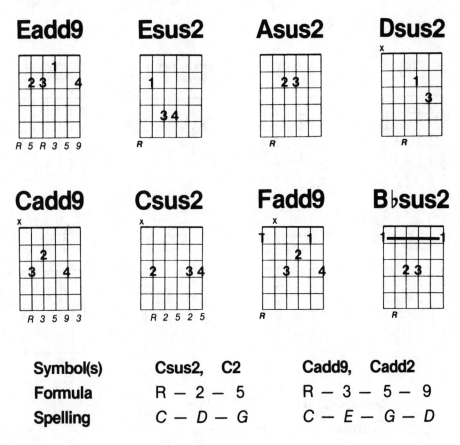

Symbol(s)	Csus2, C2	Cadd9, Cadd2
Formula	R — 2 — 5	R — 3 — 5 — 9
Spelling	C — D — G	C — E — G — D

Figure 18-11

The minor major7, written Cm(M7), Cm(♮7), or Cm(♯7), is a minor triad with the 7th degree of the major scale: root, flat 3rd, 5th, 7th. The minor major7 is used as a passing chord between the minor triad and minor7, as in "Stairway to Heaven" (Led Zeppelin) and "Michelle" (the Beatles).

Extensions and Alterations of Seventh Chords

Chord types with numbers higher than 7 are seventh chords with added scale tones. For example, C9 is a C7 chord with the added 9th degree, D. Similarly, CMaj9 is a CMaj7 with an added D note, and Cm9 is a Cm7 with an added D.

The ninth chords contain five different notes each. When voicing higher extensions, the guitarist must often leave out some notes. The 3rd and 7th degrees should not be dropped. The 3rd specifies the major or minor quality of a chord; the 7th, if flatted, specifies the dominant quality. The highest scale degree specified by the chord type should also be included.

Dominant Ninths

The dominant ninth is an extension of the dominant seventh. Not all the shapes in Figure 18–12 include the root of the chord.

Figure 18–13 shows C9 used in several different styles. Example *a* is a fingerpicking

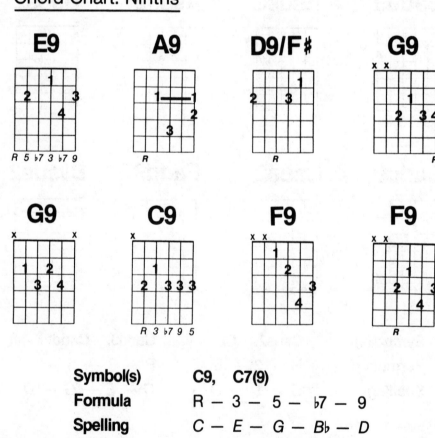

Chord Chart: Ninths

Symbol(s)	C9, C7(9)
Formula	R — 3 — 5 — ♭7 — 9
Spelling	C — E — G — B♭ — D

Figure 18-12

Vamps on C9 (Varied Styles)

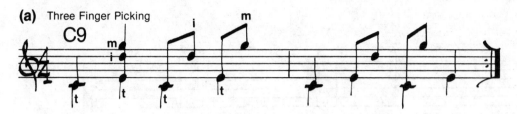

(a) Three Finger Picking

(b) Bass/Chord Strumming

(c) Rhythm and Blues

(d) Samba

Figure 18-13

pattern. Example *b* is a flatpicking strumming pattern. Example *c* is a rhythm and blues riff. Example *d* is a typical samba or bossa nova pattern. The thumb plays the bass notes, and the index, middle, and ring fingers play the treble string chords. Ninth chords are also used in the sixteenth note mute and squeeze strumming pattern in Figure 11–10.

Major and Minor Ninths

The Maj9 is an extension of the Maj7. To play a major ninth chord, add the ninth degree of the scale to a major s eventh chord. The minor 9th is an extension of the minor 7th. To play a minor ninth chord, add the ninth degree of the scale to a minor seventh chord.

Vamps on C9 (Tab)

(a) C9

(b)

(c)

(d)

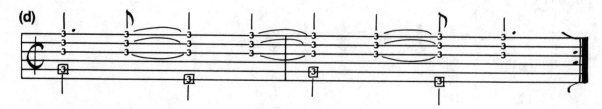

Figure 18-14

Chord Chart: Major Ninths

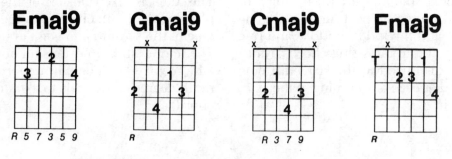

Emaj9	**Gmaj9**	**Cmaj9**	**Fmaj9**

Symbol(s)	C Maj9, CM9, C△9
Formula	R — 3 — 5 — 7 — 9
Spelling	C — E — G — B — D

Figure 18-15

Chord Chart: Minor Ninths

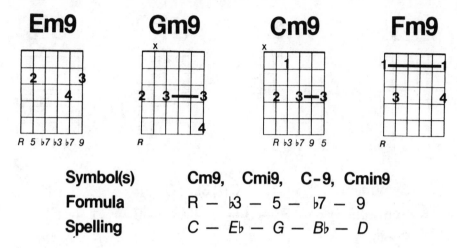

Symbol(s)	Cm9, Cmi9, C-9, Cmin9
Formula	R — b3 — 5 — b7 — 9
Spelling	C — Eb — G — Bb — D

Figure 18-16

Dominant Elevenths and Thirteenths

The eleventh chord is formed by adding the 9th and 11th degrees of the scale to the seventh chord. The thirteenth chord is formed by adding the 9th, 11th, and 13th degrees.

Figure 18–19 shows shapes for IIm7—V7 progressions with extensions. The chords are voiced so that they share notes. In *a,* Am11 and D7 have the same notes ex- cept for the note on the fourth string. In *b,* the flat 3rd of Dm9 is the same note as the flat 7th of G13; the 9th of Dm9 is the same as the 13th of G13.

Extensions of IIm7—V7 chord progres- sion can be heard in "Mr. Magic" by Grover Washington, Jr., and in Boz Scaggs' "Low Down." The sound of minor and dominant eleventh chords can also be heard in "Isn't She Lovely" (Stevie Wonder) and "Moon- dance" (Van Morrison).

Chord Chart: Elevenths

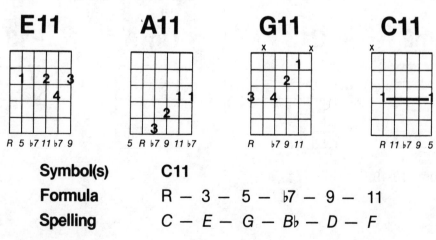

Symbol(s)	C11
Formula	R — 3 — 5 — b7 — 9 — 11
Spelling	C — E — G — Bb — D — F

Figure 18-17

Chord Chart: Thirteenths

E13

R 5 ♭7 3 13 R

A13

5 R ♭7 9 3 13

G13

R ♭7 3 13 9

C13

R 3 ♭7 9 13

Symbol(s)	C13, C7(13), C7(6)
Formula	R − 3 − 5 − ♭7 − 9 − 11 − 13
Spelling	C − E − G − B♭ − D − F − A

Figure 18-18

Extensions of **IIm7 V7**

(a)

Am11

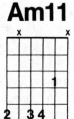

D7

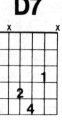

(b)

Dm9

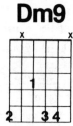

G13

(c)

Gm9

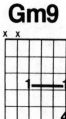

C13

(d)

Cm9

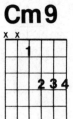

F13

Figure 18-19

Altered Seventh Chords

Altered chord are voiced by raising or lowering notes in a dominant seventh chord or its extension. For example, C7♭5♯9 is voiced by lowering the 5th degree and raising the 9th a half step each.

Altered chords are used extensively in jazz but also appear in the rock repertoire. The 7♯9 chord appears in "Foxy Lady" and "Purple Haze" by Jimi Hendrix, and also in "Taxman" by the Beatles. The Police's "Murder by Numbers" uses many altered chord shapes.

Half Diminished Sevenths

The half diminished seventh is also called a minor seventh flat five (m7♭5). The m7♭5, minor sixth, and dominant ninth chords are synonyms, as shown in Figure 18–21. The first grid shows the names of notes on a chord shape. The remaining grids show how these notes function in a G9, Bm7♭5, or Dm6 chord. Any ninth chord voiced without a root is also a shape for a m7♭5 or a minor sixth chord. For example, the top four strings of the C9 chord in Figure 18–12 contain the same notes as Gm6 and Em7♭5.

Chord Chart: Altered Sevenths

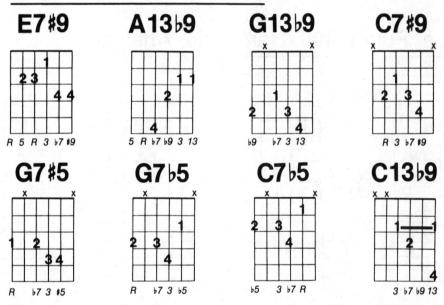

Figure 18-20

Functional Analysis of Chords

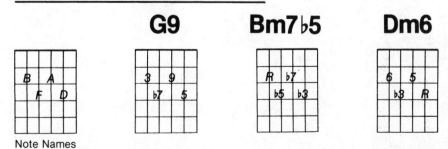

Note Names in a Chord Shape

Harmonic Function of Notes with Different Chord Names/Roots

Figure 18-21

The Diminished Seventh

The diminished seventh chord is spelled with the root, flat 3rd, flat 5th, and double flatted 7th degrees of the major scale. The double flatted seventh, or diminished seventh degree, is the same note as the 6th. Every note of the diminished seventh chord is a root: Cdim7 = E♭dim7 = Adim7.

Diminished seventh chord shapes are formed by lowering the flat 7th degree of half diminished chord shapes a half step. Diminished seventh chords are also formed by lowering the 5th degree of a minor sixth chord, or lowering by a half step the 9th degree of a dominant ninth chord voiced without a root. The diminished seventh is a syn-onym for the dominant 7♭9 a half step below: E♭dim7 = D7♭9.

Exercises and Projects

1. Know the spelling and harmonic functions (scale degree) of the notes in every chord you play.

2. Figure 18–22a shows a single chord shape with four different names. The chord at *a* is Gm7, B♭6, C11, or E♭M9. Scale degrees under the grid show how the notes function in each chord name. Name the chord types for all the given roots in *b, c,* and *d.* Show how each note functions in the chords.

Exercise: Functional (Harmonic) Analysis

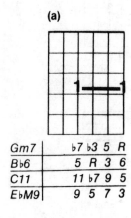 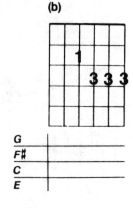 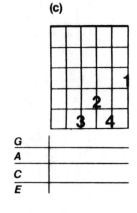 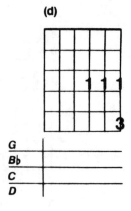

(a)

Gm7	♭7 ♭3 5 R
B♭6	5 R 3 6
C11	11 ♭7 9 5
E♭M9	9 5 7 3

(b)

G	
F♯	
C	
E	

(c)

G	
A	
C	
E	

(d)

G	
B♭	
C	
D	

19

TOPICS IN MUSIC THEORY

Three-Part Harmony

Triads

Figure 19–1 shows a harmonized C major scale. Each stack of three notes is called a triad. The low notes in each group form the C major scale, from root C to C one octave higher. The middle note of each triad is a third above the scale note. The highest note of each triad is a 3rd above the middle note, and at the same time, a 5th above the low note.

There are two ways to name the chords in Figure 19–1:

1. Locate the notes of each triad on the major scale named by the lowest note. For example, the first chord, C—E—G, is a C major triad because C, E, and G are the root, 3rd, and 5th of the C scale. The notes of the second chord, D—F—A, are the root, flat 3rd, and 5th of the D major scale, or a D minor triad.

2. Look at the intervals between the notes of each triad. A major triad is a minor third above a major third. A minor triad is a major third above a minor third.

Chords of the Key

The chords in Figure 19–1 are the chords of the key of C. The pattern of chord types produced by harmonization of the C major scale applies to all major scales.

Knowing the pattern of chords of the key is useful for songwriters who need to harmonize a melody, for players and arrangers who use chord substitutions, for improvisers who solo over chord changes, and for guitarists who learn songs by ear.

Figure 19–2a shows the chords of the key of C. Line *b* shows the formula for the chords of the key for all major scales. The roman numerals correspond to the scale degrees. The chord type associated with each scale degree is the same for every key. Line *c* shows the chords of the key of G. The roots of the chords are the notes of the G major scale.

The Minor Seventh Flat Five Chord

The chord constructed on the seventh degree of the major scale is a minor chord with a flatted fifth degree (m7♭5), or diminished triad. The VII diminished triad is best understood as the dominant seventh built on

Triads: C Major Harmonized in Thirds

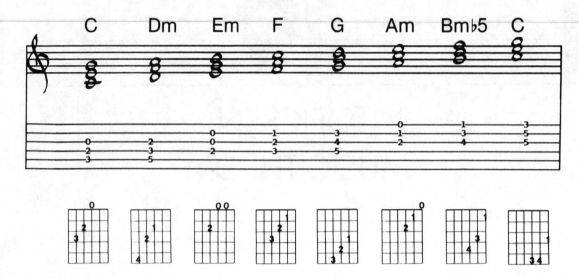

Figure 19-1

Chords of the Key

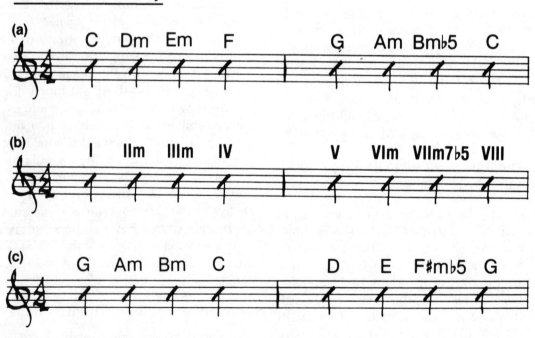

Figure 19-2

the fifth degree (V7), voiced with no root. The notes of the B diminished triad, B—D—F, are the 3rd, 5th, and flat 7th of G.

The chords of the key contain three majors (I, IV, and V), three minors (IIm, IIIm, VIm) and one dominant seventh chord, V7, disguised as the VII diminished chord.

Inversions

Every interval has an inversion. The inversion of an interval is formed by raising the lower note an octave so that it sounds above the higher note. Understanding inversions helps the guitarist to organize and understand chord construction, voicings, shapes, and fingerings. The study of inversions also helps the guitarists locate patterns of intervals on the guitar. Knowing patterns of intervals is useful for improvising and arranging.

Inversions of Major Scale Intervals

C to E is a major 3rd. Raising the pitch of C an octave yields the inversion E to C, as shown in Figure 19–3. The interval from E to C is a minor 6th. The intervals C to E (major third) and E to C (minor sixth) are inversions of each other.

An Interval and Its Inversion

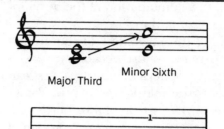

Major Third   Minor Sixth

Figure 19-3

The following are the rules of inversions:

1. An interval plus its inversion adds up to nine. For example, the inversion of a 3rd is a 6th (3+6=9). The inversion of a 4th is a 5th (4+5=9).
2. When intervals are inverted, major intervals become minor and minor intervals become major. Augmented and diminished intervals likewise trade places, and perfect intervals remain perfect.

Inversions of Chords

A chord is inverted by raising its lowest note to a higher octave. Figure 19–4 shows three inversions of a C major triad. The chord in

Inversions of **C** Major Triad

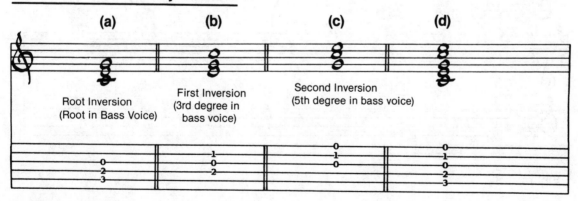

(a) Root Inversion (Root in Bass Voice)

(b) First Inversion (3rd degree in bass voice)

(c) Second Inversion (5th degree in bass voice)

(d)

Figure 19-4

Figure 19–4d is a common C major chord in first position, a combination of the three inversions in *a*, *b*, and *c*.

Learning the inversions of the chords of the key expands chord vocabulary, develops left hand dexterity, improves the ear, and educates the mind. Figure 19–5 shows first and second inversion of the chords of C major. Each inversion is shown on one set of strings. Other shapes are possible.

The chords in Figure 19–5 are examples of *close voicing*. A close voicing of a chord is a structure made up of notes which are close together in pitch. An *open voicing*

of a chord is made up of notes which are farther apart.

Four-part Harmony

Harmonizing scales in four parts produces the *diatonic seventh chords*, shown in Figure 19–6. The sequence of four-part chord types created by harmonizing the C major scale holds true for all major scales.

Figure 19–7 shows an open voicing and practical fingering of diatonic seventh chords in C major.

First and Second Inversions of Chords of Key in C

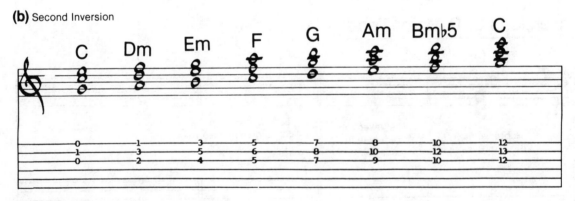

Figure 19-5

Four Part Harmonization of C Major

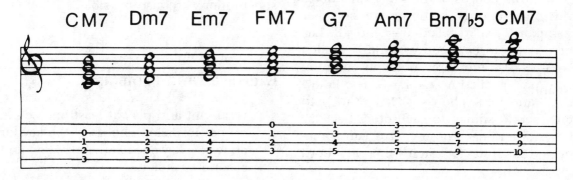

Figure 19-6

Diatonic Seventh Chords

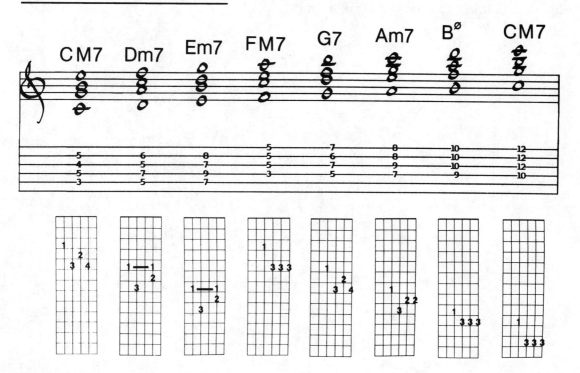

Figure 19-7

Chord Substitution

Each of the chords of the key shares notes with other chords in the progression. For example, CMaj7, spelled C—E—G—B, has three notes in common with Em7, spelled E—G—B—D, and three notes in common with Am7, spelled A—C—E—G. The IMaj7, IIIm7, and VIm7 chords (CMaj7, Em7, and Am7) sound similar to each other because they share notes. These chords can sometimes substitute for each other in chord progressions.

Diatonic sevenths have one of three sounds: *tonic*, *sub-dominant*, and *dominant*. The tonic chords are IMaj7, IIIm7, and VIm7. Sub-dominant chords are the IIm7 and IVMaj7. The dominant chords are V7, VIIm7♭5, and IIIm7. Chords which are in the same sound grouping can substitute for each other in chord progressions. Other substitutions are also possible.

Exercises and Projects

1. Write out and play at least one octave of root inversion chords of the key for all twelve keys. Similarly, play first and second inversions.

2. Verify that the chord types for diatonic seventh chords shown in Figure 19–7 are correct. Memorize the pattern of chord types.

3. Play diatonic sevenths in all twelve keys.

20

SOLO GUITAR: FINGERSTYLE

Charlie Byrd, Joe Pass, Laurindo Almeida, Guy Van Duser, Chet Atkins, Carlos Barbosa-Lima, Leo Brouwer, Marcel Dadi, Eric Schoenberg, Lenny Breau, Ralph Towner, Andrew Schulman and many other guitarists perform and record their own fingerstyle arrangements of folk, popular, and jazz melodies.

With the musical and guitar playing skills developed through studying the material in this book, and with the sheet music of a favorite song, a guitarist can create an individual fingerpicking solo style arrangement. The widespread availability of sheet music offers a diverse range of songs for the creative arranger and player to explore.

The Classical Heritage

Even if guitarists are interested and skilled in only the techniques of contemporary music, they should not overlook the wealth of helpful material in the repertoire of the classical guitar. The following overview places the classical guitar in perspective for the contemporary musician.

Monophonic, Polyphonic, and Homophonic Music

Musical styles fall into one of three categories: monophony, homophony, and polyphony. Unaccompanied melody, or monophony, is the oldest form of music. Monophony is found throughout the world's folk music.

Polyphonic music is a combination of several simultaneous melody lines in which each voice has an independent and equal existence. Polyphony reached its zenith in the eighteenth-century Baroque counterpoint of J. S. Bach.

Homophonic music is composed of several voices in which a single melody line enjoys supremacy. The subordinant voices support the melody and form chords. These chords establish a pulse or follow the melody. Most nineteenth-century classical music is homophonic. The sonatas and symphonies of Beethoven, the operas and quartets of Mozart, and the masterpieces of Chopin are known for their great themes or melodies.

The early nineteenth century witnessed the first significant period of composition and virtuoso performance on the six string guitar. Naturally, the nineteenth-century guitarists — Sor, Carcassi, Aguado, Giuliani, and Tárrega—wrote in homophonic style, melodies with accompaniments. *Etudes* by these composers are available at music stores. Each etude offers an exercise in guitar technique and a lesson in arranging melodies and chords.

Blues, Stride, Ragtime, and Rock

The guitar became popular on an unprecedented level in the 1950s and 1960s. The first generation of rock and roll, the folk boom, the Beatles, and quantum advances in the technology of sound recording and amplification spurred widespread interest and participation in guitar music.

As guitarists began to explore the roots of folk and popular music, they discovered players from earlier eras who had developed new techniques and styles of guitar playing. The synthesis in the 1930s of blues, stride, and jazz idioms by the Reverend Gary Davis, Willie Johnson, Mississippi John Hurt, and others inspired guitarists to transpose ragtime piano pieces and traditional fiddle and banjo tunes to the guitar. The tradition of creating original arrangements of popular songs on the guitar continues to the present day.

Creating an Arrangement

The experienced guitarist can sometimes play an arrangement of a melody by sight or by ear. If necessary, follow each step in the process. As you gain experience you can omit some of the steps or perform them solely in your mind.

Steps to Creating an Arrangement

Confine the melody to the treble strings so that a bass line and intermediate voices can be added below it. It is easier to combine a melody with bass lines and chords if some chord notes fall on open strings. Transpose to a key that uses at least some open strings. There are usually several good choices of keys.

1. Write down the melody and chords.
2. Analyze the melody and chord progression.
3. Transpose to an appropriate key, if necessary.
4. Add a bass line to the melody.
5. Harmonize the melody in thirds, sixths, or tenths.
6. Fill in the space between the bass line and melody with harmonies implied by the chord progression.
7. Use extensions and alterations of chord synonyms and substitutions to create new harmonies.
8. Where possible, add melodic licks and fills based on the melody, chord changes, or popular recordings of the song.
9. Vary the texture and density of the arrangement.

In this section, the steps to creating an arrangement are illustrated with the famous "Ode to Joy" theme from Beethoven's Ninth Symphony and a solo guitar arrangement of "Georgia on My Mind." Figure 20–1 shows sixteen measures of the Beethoven melody in the original key.

The roots of the chords are written below the melody on the first beat of each chord change. Bass notes in this arrangement fall on open strings. Play bass notes with the thumb and melody notes with the index and middle fingers.

The key of D is very appealing because of the open string root notes. On the other hand, D may not be the best key when harmonies, inner voices, and chord substitutions are used. The only way to tell which key is the most satisfying is to write and play arrangements in several keys.

Ode to Joy: Melody with Simple Bass

by Ludwig Van Beethoven

Figure 20-1

Ode to Joy: Melody with Simple Bass (Tab)

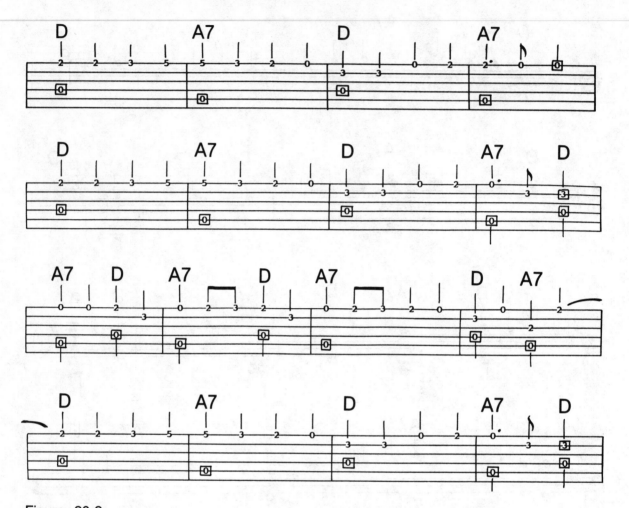

Figure 20-2

Harmonizing the Melody

Use the patterns of major scales harmonized in 3rds, 6ths, and 10ths. Keep the melody line as the highest voice in a harmony. Figure 20–3a shows four measures of the melody transposed to C and harmonized in 3rds. Figure 20–3b is the melody in 6ths. The measures in *c* contain 10ths, 6ths, 3rds, and other intervals.

Choose harmony notes which enhance the chord changes. Avoid changes between harmonies which distract from the melody; the harmony should follow the contour of the melody. Avoid harmonies which conflict with significant notes in the accompanying chords.

Melody with Mixed Intervals

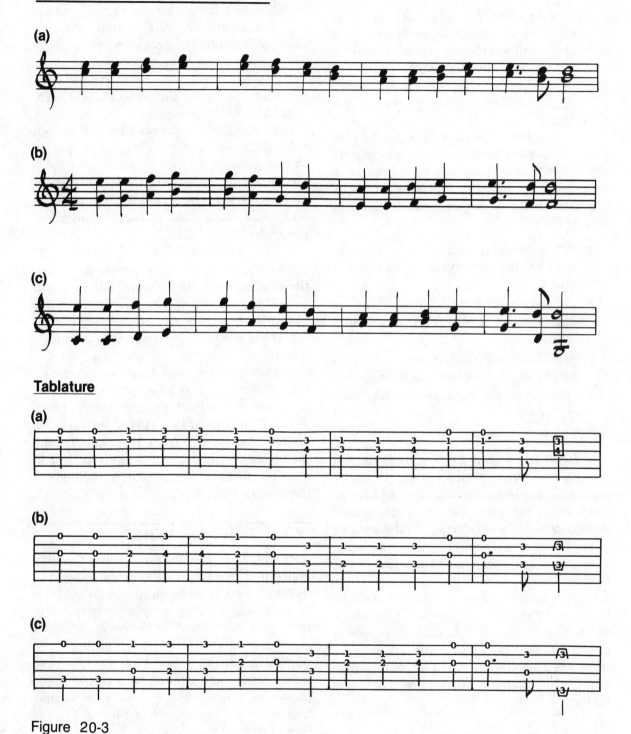

Tablature

Figure 20-3

The Bass Line

Next to the melody, the bass line is the most important voice in an arrangement. The bass line supports the melody and outlines or hints at the chord changes. The bass voice should refer to the melody and chord changes and still enjoy its own internal musical logic.

A bass line consisting of repeated root notes, or which follows every melody note with the same interval, soon becomes tedious to the ear. The following concepts are used in the arrangement in C major in Figure 20–4.

1. *Parallel motion*, bass lines that rise and fall with the melody, as in measures 1 and 2.
2. *Contrary motion*, bass lines that move opposite the melody, as in measures 3 and 14.
3. *Ascending and descending scale fragments*, as in measures 13 through 15.
4. *Lines that fall on chord tones* (very common).
5. *Chromatic scales*, as in measure 10.

The bass line begins by harmonizing the melody in 10ths. A descending C major scale passage begins on the second beat of the second measure, and turns into a four note chromatic scale starting on the second beat of measure three. The last three beats of measure four comprise an arpeggio of the G major triad.

The first ten bass notes are repeated starting at the fifth measure, with a change in rhythm. Measure 7 begins with two C chord notes. The short scale passage in measure 7 begins on the open sixth string and forms diatonic thirteenths with the melody.

Arrangement with Picking Patterns

Figures 20–6 through 20–9 show an arrangement of the Beethoven theme using three fingerpicking patterns. As with accompaniments, picking patterns are made more interesting by adding bass lines and bass runs.

The arrangement is written with note durations doubled to make reading easier. The melody is sometimes syncopated by delaying it half a beat, as in the first and third measures, or by striking it half a beat early, as in the ninth measure.

In the first four measures, the melody is harmonized in various intervals while the thumb plays alternating bass patterns. A chromatically ascending bass line starting on open string E begins in the fifth measure and turns into a diatonic bass run in measure eight.

The alternating bass in measures 10 through 13 follows an irregular pattern. Play the bass notes separately to hear its logic.

The descending bass line in measures 13 and 14 echoes the ascending line in measures 6 and 7. Measure 15 is a calypso picking pattern wth syncopated bass notes.

The counterpoint bass line in measures 21 through 24 is adapted from the oboe and clarinet parts in the Beethoven score.

D.C. al coda at the end of measure 23 is an indication to return to the beginning. Repeat from the first measure until the brackets after measure 6, then skip to the coda at the end of the piece.

"Georgia on My Mind"

Each measure of this arrangement uses a concept or technique that can be applied to the entire song or to other melodies. The arrangement can be simplified by playing only the bass and melody notes. The arrangement can be further simplified by playing the melody and only the first bass note under each chord. In the first eight measures, with a few exceptions, the first bass note under each chord is the root of that chord.

The song is structured in groups of eight-measure phrases. The progression and melody in the first and second eight bars are essentially the same. The seventh

Melody and Bass Line

Figure 20-4
©1985 by Barry Pollack.

and eighth measures of each verse is a two bar *turnaround,* a musical breathing space used to prepare for repetition of the melody. Measures 17 to 24 are a *bridge* with new melody and chords. The last eight measures have the same chords and melody as the first eight, except that an improvised melody and harmony hint at the theme. In some measures chord names are simplified to make the music more legible. These are the highlights of the arrangement:

Measures 1—4: Melody is harmonized in sixths and thirds; bass line plays mostly chord notes.

Measure 5: Color tones added to C chord; parallel movement of voices.

Measure 6: Chromatic bass line comes from chord progression.

Measure 9: Bass line on the sixth string is in opposite direction to the bass line in measure 1.

Ode to Joy (Bass Line Arrangement, Tab)

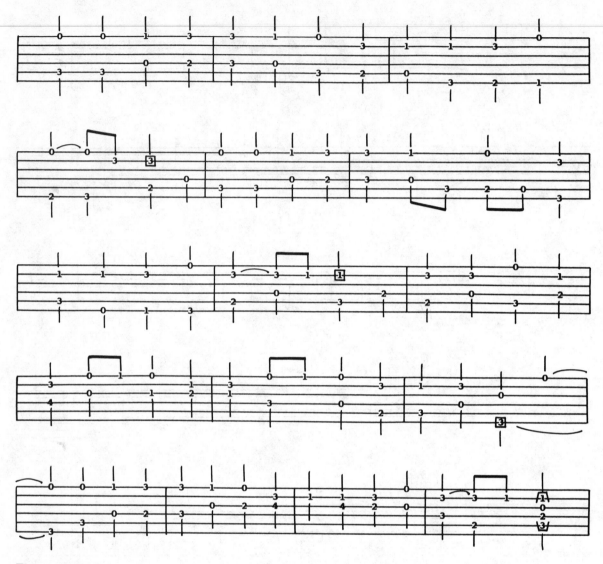

Figure 20-5
©1985 by Barry Pollack.

Measure 10: B♭7 is a tritone substitution for E7.

Measure 13: A variation on measure 5.

Measure 14: The flat 9th in the bass voice of the last chord creates a short chromatic scale.

Measures 15 and 16: The chords of the turnaround can also be arpeggiated. Chromatic sixths lead into the bridge.

Measures 17 — 21: Sustain the melody notes as long as possible.

Measure 22: The harmonies here and in measures 5 and 13 are interchangeable.

Measure 26: The two chords are the same shape.

Measures 29 and 30: Treble voice is an improvisation which outlines the chord changes.

Three Finger Picking Arrangement

Figure 20-6
©1985 by Barry Pollack.

Three Finger Picking Arrangement (Continued)

Figure 20-7

Ode to Joy (Finger Picking Arrangement, Tab)

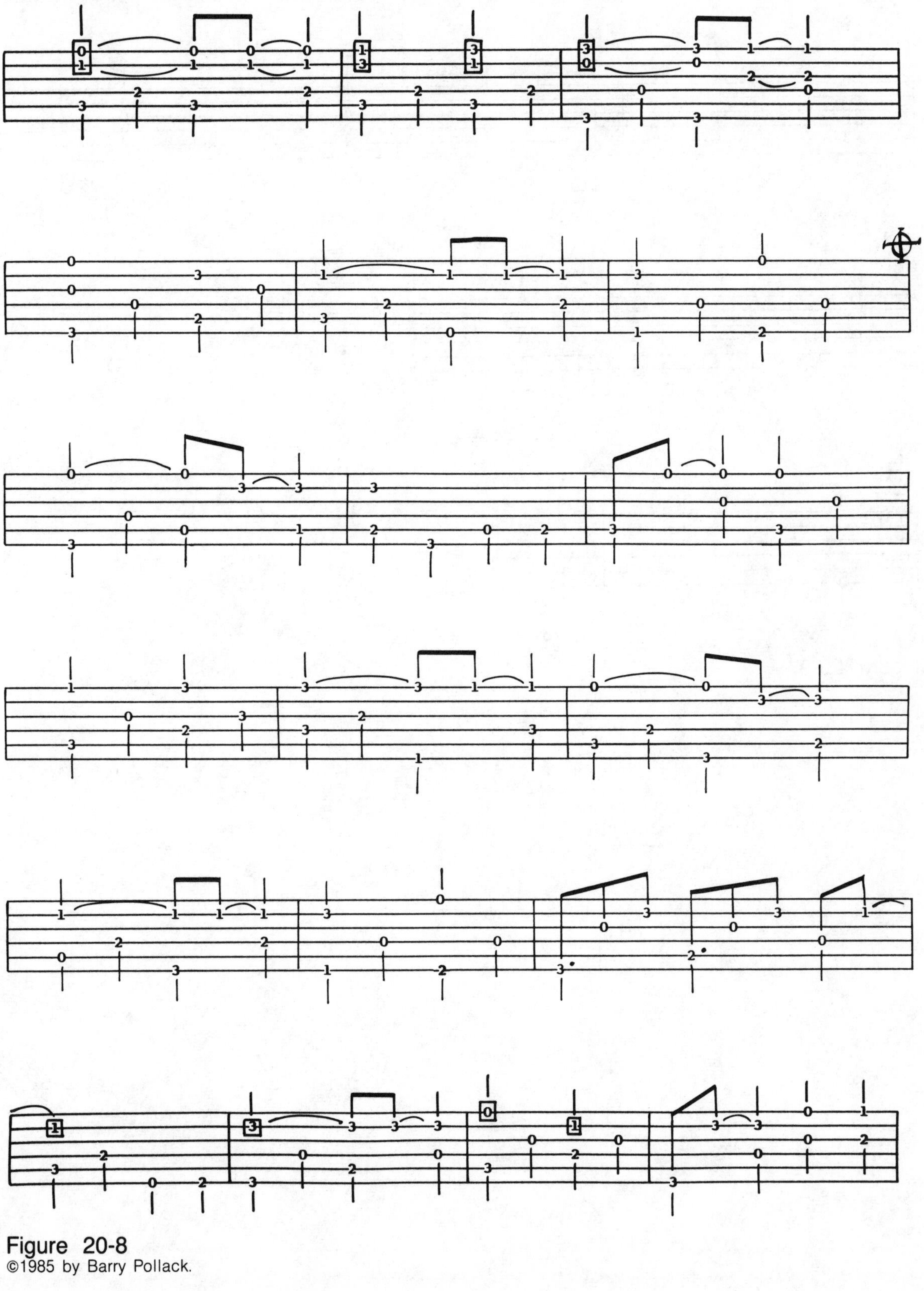

Figure 20-8
©1985 by Barry Pollack.

Three Finger Picking Arrangement (Continued, Tab)

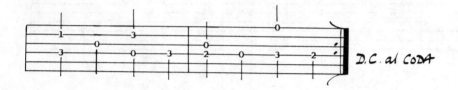

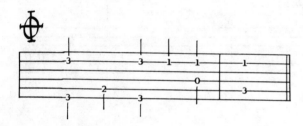

Figure 20-9

Georgia On My Mind
(Finger Style Solo Arrangement)

Arranged for guitar by Barry Pollack
Music by Hoagy Carmichael, Lyrics by Stuart Gorrell

Figure 20-10

Georgia on My Mind (Continued)

Figure 20-11

Georgia On My Mind (Tab)

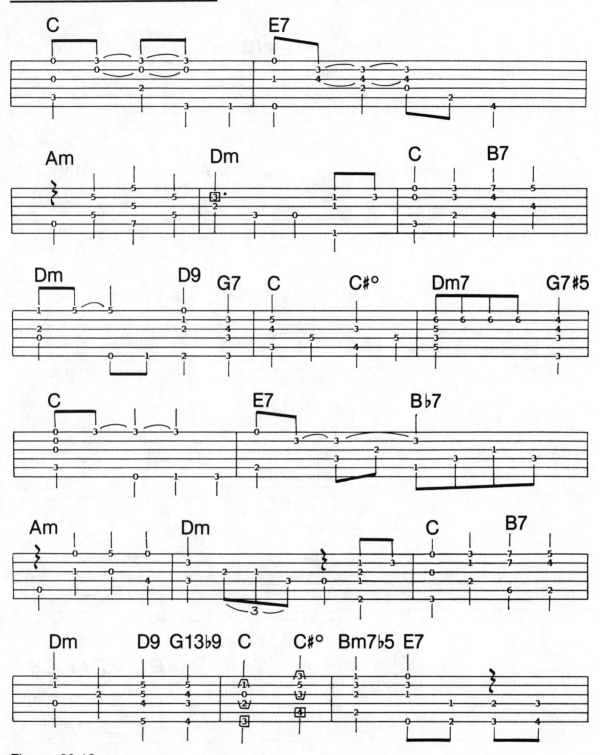

Figure 20-12

Georgia on My Mind (Continued, Tab)

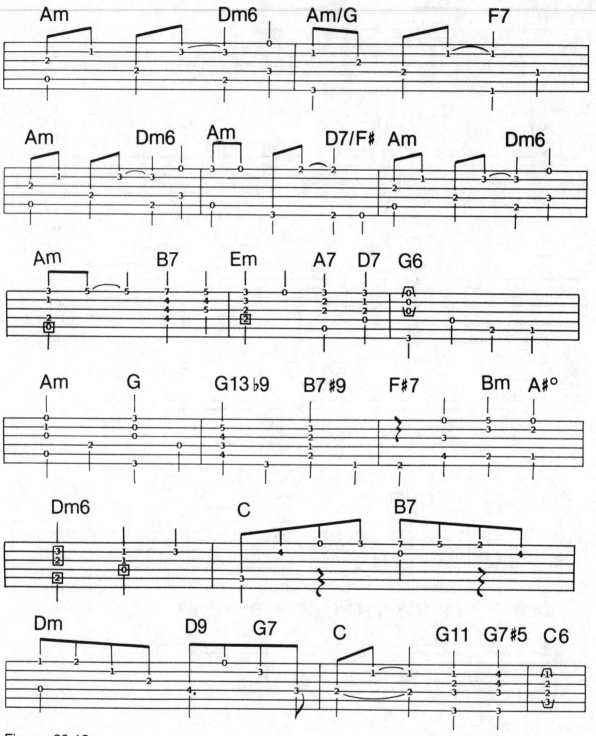

Figure 20-13

Suggestions for Further Study

Arranging on the guitar is an art of the possible. Not all chord voicings or bass notes can be reached by four fingers on six strings. The arranger first must learn what notes to play and then must learn what notes to omit.

Learn to read music well. Almost all pop tunes are available in sheet music with piano arrangements. You can use the printed piano parts as a source of ideas for creating your own guitar arrangements. Keep trying to copy licks and guitar parts from recordings. A few recognizable riffs go a long way to making an arrangement appealing to the listener.

Practice the classical guitar etudes described in the beginning of this chapter. Opus numbers and publishers are listed in the bibliography. Listen to recordings of other solo guitar arrangers.

Listen to a lounge or piano bar pianist. Observe how the artist arranges melodies.

Imagine how you could produce the same sound on the guitar. Request the pianist to play a song which you are trying to arrange on guitar. Leave a tip for the musician.

Exercises and Projects

1. Rewrite sixteen measures of the Beethoven melody in the keys of C, A, and G. Visualize how the melody notes are played within different voicings and chord shapes in each key.
2. Play sixteen measures of the melody harmonized in 3rds, 6ths, and 10ths in the keys of C, D, G, and A. Add root bass notes where possible.
3. Write down several bass lines for the melody.
4. How do the notes in "Georgia on My Mind" function in each chord?
5. Write your own arrangements of these or other melodies.

AFTERWORD

Wherever possible, musical concepts and guitar playing techniques have been illustrated with transcriptions of recorded and well-known guitar parts. More complete transcriptions and titles could not be included due to budget, space, and editorial limitations. The serious student or teacher is encouraged to seek out recordings or sheet music of the titles referred to in order to understand better the concepts and techniques discussed.

I wish to thank again the publishers of the songs that appear in this book.

Bibliography
History, Biography Criticism, and General Interest

Bernstein, Leonard. *The Unanswered Question.* Harvard University Press, Cambridge, 1976.

Brown, Charles T. *The Art of Rock and Roll.* Prentice-Hall, Inc., Englewood Cliffs, NJ, 1983.

Gillett, Charlie. *The Sound of the City: The Rise of Rock and Roll.* Dell, New York, 1972.

Grunfeld, Frederick. *The Art and Times of the Guitar: An Illustrated History of Guitars and Guitarists.* Macmillan, New York, 1969.

————. *Lost Highway: Journeys and Arrivals of American Musicians.* David R. Godine, Boston, 1979.

Guralnik, Peter. *Feel Like Going Home: Portraits in Blues and Rock'n'Roll.* Vintage Books, New York, 1981.

Holt, John. *Never Too Late: My Musical Life Story.* Dell, New York, 1978.

Kozinn, Allan, et al. *The Guitar. The History. The Music. The Players.* Quill, New York, 1984.

Marcus, Greil. *Mystery Train: Images of America in Rock'n'Roll Music.* E.P. Dutton, New York, 1982 (revised).

Miller, Jim, Ed. *The Rolling Stone History of Rock and Roll.* Rolling Stone Press, New York, 1976.

Palmer, Robert. *Deep Blues.* Viking Press, New York, 1981.

Palmer, Tony. *Julian Bream: A Life on the Road.* Franklin Watts, New York, 1983.

Rockwell, John. *All American Music: Composition in the Late Twentieth Century.* Alfred A. Knopf, New York, 1983.

Sagan, Carl, et al. *Murmurs of Earth: The Voyager Interstellar Record.* Ballantine Books, New York, 1978.

Sallis, James. *The Guitar Players: One Instrument and Its Masters in American Music.* Quill, New York, 1982.

Stokes, Geoffrey. *Starmaking Machinery: Inside the Business of Rock and Roll.* Vintage Books, New York, 1977.

Vulliamy, Graham, and Lee, Ed. *Pop Music in School.* Cambridge University Press, 1976.

————. *Pop, Rock, and Ethnic Music in School.* Cambridge University Press, 1982.

Instruction Books—Varied Styles

Barenberg, Russ. *Clarence White Guitar.* Oak Publications, New York, 1978.

Berle, Arnie. *Arnie Berle's Book of Modern Chords and Progressions for Guitar.* Amsco Music Publishing Company, Ann Arbor, MI, 1968.

Carcassi, Matteo. (Edited and Fingered by Frederick Noad.) *25 Melodic and Progressive Studies, Opus 60,* Ariel Publications, New York, 1977.

Coker, Jerry. *Improvising Jazz.* Prentice-Hall, Inc., Englewood Cliffs, NJ, 1964.

Giuliani, Mauro. *24 Etudes, Opus 48.* Schott Music Corp., New York, 1970.

Grossman, Stefan. *Ragtime Blues Guitarists.* Oak Publications, New York, 1970.

————. *Delta Blues Guitar.* Oak Publications, New York, 1969.

————. *Rev. Gary Davis/Blues Guitar.* Oak Publications, New York, 1974.

Ihde, Mike. *Country Guitar Styles.* Berklee Press Publications, Boston, 1979.

———. *Rock Guitar Styles.* Berklee Press Publications, Boston, 1981.

Jeffery, Brian, Ed. *Aguado: New Guitar Method.* Tecla Editions, London, 1981.

Leavett, William G. *A Modern Method for Guitar, 3 Vols.* Berklee Press Publications, Boston, 1966.

Mock, Don, Ed. *Ten Top Guitarists Offer Their Insights to Guitar Artistry.* Musicians Institute Publications, Inc., Hollywood, 1982.

Morgan, Howard. *Preparations: An Introduction to Fingerstyle Playing.* The Big 3 Music Corporation, New York, 1982.

Concepts: Arranging for Fingerstyle Guitar. The Big 3 Music Corporation, New York, 1982.

Noad, Fred. *Solo Guitar Playing, Books One and Two: A Complete Course of Instructions in the Techniques of Guitar Performance.* Macmillan, New York, 1968.

Pass, Joe. *Joe Pass Guitar Style.* Gwyn Publishing Co., Sherman Oaks, California, 1970.

Perlman, Ken. *Fingerstyle Guitar.* Prentice-Hall, Inc., Englewood Cliffs, NJ, 1980.

Roth, Arlen. *How to Play Blues Guitar.* Acorn Music Press, New York, 1976.

———. *Traditional, Country, and Electric Slide Guitar.* Oak Publications, New York, 1975.

———. *Nashville Guitar.* Oak Publications, New York, 1977.

Segovia, Andres. *Diatonic Scales.* Columbia Music Company, Washington, D.C., 1953.

Segovia, Andres, Ed. *Studies for the Guitar by Fernando Sor.* Edward B. Marks Corporation, Melville, NY, 1965.

Tarrega, Francisco, Karl Scheit, Ed. *Complete Technical Studies.* Universal Edition, Vienna, 1969.

Traum, Happy. *Traditional and Contemporary Guitar Fingerpicking Styles.* Oak Publications, New York, 1969.

———. *Fingerpicking Styles for Guitar.* Oak Publications, New York, 1980 (revised).

———. *Homespun Tapes.* Homespun Tapes Ltd., Box 694, New York, NY 12498.

Transcriptions

Knowles, John. *Jerry Reed Heavy Neckin'.* Sound Hole, Nashville, 1980.

Atkins, Chet. *Chet Atkins Note-for-Note.* Guitar Player Productions, Saratoga, CA, 1975.

Ayeroff, Stan. *Jazz Masters: Charlie Christian.* Consolidated Music Publishers, New York, 1979.

———. *Wes Montgomery, Jazz Guitar Solos.* Almo Publications, Hollywood, 1976.

Barker, Mick. *Steve Howe Guitar Pieces.* Warner Bros. Publications, New York, 1980.

Doctor Licks. *Doctor Licks Vols. One through Six.* Doctor Licks, 327 Haverford Road, Wynnewood, PA 19096.

Gleason, James. *Note-for-Note Guitar Solos.* Rock Performance Music Co., Berkeley, CA.

Sokolow, Fred. *Giants of Rock Guitar.* Almo Publications, Hollywood, 1978.

Magazines

Frets. GPI Publications, Cupertino, CA.

Guitar Player Magazine. GPI Publications, Cupertino, CA.

Guitar Review. Rose L. Augustine, New York.

Guitar for the Practicing Musician. Cherry Lane Music, Port Chester, NY.

Musician. Amordian Press, Gloucester, MA.

Reference Books

Apel, Willi, Ed. *Harvard Dictionary of Music, Second Edition, Revised 2nd Enlarged.* Cambridge, MA, 1972.

Marsh, Dave, and Stein, Dave. *The Book of Rock Lists.* Dell, New York, 1981.

Seigmeister, Elie. *Harmony and Melody. Volume I, The Diatonic Style. Volume 2, Modulation: Chromaticism and Modern Styles.* Wadsworth Publishing Company, Inc., Belmont, CA, 1965.

APPENDIX B

Discography

The following list of recordings are the primary sources from which the transcribed riffs, rhythms, and solos were learned. Many of the songs can also be heard in "best of" collections and other reissues. For complete lists of recorded guitar styles, see the excellent published discographies in Charles T. Brown's *The Art of Rock and Roll*, and Graham Vulliamy and Edward Lee's *Pop Music in Schools* and *Popular Music: A Teacher's Guide*. The magazines *Guitar Player* and *Guitar for the Practicing Musician* occasionally list historically significant recordings.

Title, Album, and Label	Figure
"Around and Around," *12 × 5* (Rolling Stones), Decca.	17–3
"Back in the USSR," *White Album*, Apple SWB 0101.	17–13
"Bad, Bad, Leroy Brown," *Life and Times*, Lifesongs LS 8002.	11–6
"Breezin," *Breezin'*, (George Benson), Warner Bros. BS 2919.	16–11
"Bring It on Home to Me," *The Best of the Animals*, MGM SE-4324.	17–7
"Brown Eyed Girl," *The Best of Van Morrison*, Bang Records 222.	16–12
"Brown Sugar," *Sticky Fingers*, Rolling Stones Records COC 59100.	18–7
"Circle Game," *Ladies of the Canyon*, Reprise 6376.	11–13
"Diamonds and Rust," *Diamonds and Rust*, A&M 4527.	6–2
"Get Back," *Let It Be*, Apple AR 34001.	17–11
"Heart of Gold," *Decade*, WB 3RS 2257.	14–4
"Homeward Bound," *Parsley, Sage, Rosemary, and Thyme*, Columbia CS9363.	16–3
"In the Midnight Hour," *The Exciting Wilson Pickett*, Atlantic 8129.	11–5
"Johnny B. Goode," *Chuck Berry's Golden Decade*, Chess 2CH1514.	17–1
"Jumping Jack Flash," *Get Yer Ya-Ya's Out* (The Rolling Stones in Concert), London NPS5.	11–12
"Landslide," *Fleetwood Mac*, Reprise MS 2225.	6–6
"Margarittaville," *Changes in Lattitudes, Changes in Attitudes*, ABC AB-990.	16–10
"Me and Bobby McGee," *Pearl* (Janis Joplin and the Full Tilt Boogie Band), Columbia KC30322.	5–2
"Me and Julio Down by the School Yard," *Paul Simon*, Columbia KC30750.	4–4
"Mr. Bojangles," *A Man Must Carry On* (live version), MCA 2 6003.	9–5
"Needle and the Damage Done, The" *Harvest*, WB MSK2277.	9–7
"Pinball Wizard," *Tommy*, MCA2-10005.	11–9
"Play with Fire," *Out of Our Heads*, London PS 429.	6–1
"Ripple," *American Beauty*, WB WS 1893.	5–8

APPENDIX C

Song Titles

Song Title	Figure
It Don't Mean a Thing (if It Ain't Got That Swing)	10–15
James Bond Theme, The	10–7
Johnny B. Goode	17–1
Jumping Jack Flash	11–12
Landslide	6–6
Margarittaville	16–10
Me and Bobby McGee	5–2
Me and Julio Down by the School Yard	4–4
Michael, Row the Boat Ashore	10–12
Mr. Bojangles	9–5
Needle and the Damage Done, The	9–7
Ode to Joy	20–1
Pinball Wizard	11–9
Play with Fire	6–1
Ripple	5–8
Sentimental Journey	10–11
She Loves You	16–15
Should I Stay or Should I Go?	4–3
Soul Man	16–21
Sound of Silence	10–14
Star Spangled Banner, The	10–13
Star Wars	10–16
Steel Guitar Rag	17–9
Suzanne	18–9
Sweet Home Alabama	14–6
Take It Easy	4–6
That'll Be the Day	17–5
This Land Is Your Land	10–8
Tired of Waiting for You	6–2
Was a Sunny Day	16–20
Wild Horses	11–8
With a Little Help From My Friends	10–9
Yesterday	9–9
You Really Got Me	4–2
You've Got To Hide Your Love Away	9–2

CREDITS

Figure	Title, Composer, and Permission Notice

16–10 *Margarittaville* by Jimmy Buffet. Copyright © 1977 Coral Reefer Music. International Copyright Secured. All Rights Reserved. Used by Permission.

16–11 *Breezin'* by Bobby Womak. Copyright © 1971, 1976 Unart Music Corporations and Tracebob Music Co. All Rights Controlled by Unart Music Corporation. All Rights Assigned by CBS Catalogue Partnership. All Rights Administered by CBS U Catalog and Tracebob Music Co. All Rights Reserved. Used by Permission. International Copyright Secured.

16–12 *Brown Eyed Girl* by Van Morrison. Copyright © 1967 WEB IV MUSIC, INC. All Rights Reserved. Used by Permission.

16–15 *She Loves You* by John Lennon and Paul McCartney. Copyright © 1963, 1964 Northern Songs Limited. All Rights for the USA and Canada controlled by Gil Music Corp., 1650 Broadway, New York, NY 10019. All Rights Reserved. Used by Permission.

16–20 *Was A Sunny Day* by Paul Simon. Copyright © 1973 Paul Simon. Used by Permission.

16–21 *Soul Man* by David Porter and Isaac Hayes. Copyright © 1967 and 1969 Almo Music Corp. and Walden Music (ASCAP). All Rights Reserved. International Copyright Secured. Used by Permission.

17–1 *Johnny B. Goode* by Chuck Berry. Copyright © 1958, ARC Music Corp., 110 East 59 Street, New York, NY 10022. Used by Permission.

17–3 *Around and Around* by Chuck Berry. Copyright © 1958, 1964 ARC Music Corp., 110 East 59 Street, New York, NY 10022. Used by Permission.

17–5 *That'll Be the Day* by Norman Petty, Buddy Holly, and Joe Allison. Copyright © 1957 MPL Communications, Inc. and Wren Music Co. International Copyright Secured. All Rights Reserved. Used by Permission.

17–7 *Bring it on Home to Me* by Sam Cooke. Copyright © 1962 by Abkco Music, Inc. International Copyright Secured. Used by Permission. All Rights Reserved.

17–9 *Steel Guitar Rag* by Leon McAuliffe. Copyright © 1944 by Bourne Co. Copyright Renewed. Used by Permission.

17–11 *Get Back* by John Lennon and Paul McCartney. Copyright © 1969 Northern Songs Limited. All rights for the United States of America, Mexico, and the Philippines controlled by Maclen Music, Inc., c/o ATV Music Corp., 6255 Sunset Blvd., Los Angeles, CA 90028. All Rights Reserved. Used by Permission.

17–13 *Back in the USSR* by John Lennon and Paul McCartney. Copyright © 1968 Northern Songs Limited. All rights for the United States of America, Mexico, and the Philippines controlled by Maclen Music, Inc., c/o ATV Music Corp., 6255 Sunset Blvd., Los Angeles, CA 90028. All Rights Reserved. Used by Permission.

18–7 *Brown Sugar* by Mick Jagger and Keith Richards. Copyright © 1971 by Abkco Music, Inc. International Copyright Secured. All Rights Reserved. Used by Permission.

18–9 *Suzanne* by Leonard Cohen. Copyright © 1966, Project Seven Music, Continental Total Media Project, Inc., 120 Charles Street, New York, NY 10014. Used by Permission.

20–10 *Georgia On My Mind* by Stuart Gorrell and Hoagy Carmichael. Copyright © 1930 (Renewed 1957, 1980) by Peer International Corporation. International Copyright Secured. All Rights Reserved. Used by Permission.